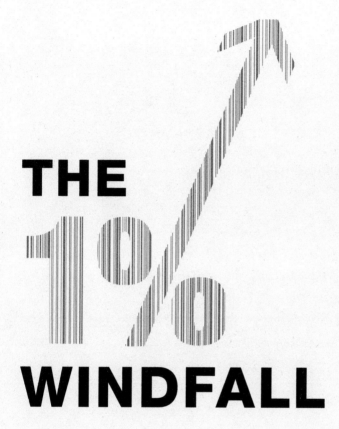

THE
1%
WINDFALL

ALSO BY RAFI MOHAMMED

The Art of Pricing

THE

1%

WINDFALL

How Successful Companies Use Price to Profit and Grow

RAFI MOHAMMED

10 Mar31
Brt
2799(1553)

1. Pricing.

HarperCollins books may be purchased for educational, business, or sales promotional use.
For information, please write: Special Markets Department, HarperCollins Publishers,
10 East 53rd Street, New York, NY 10022.

FIRST EDITION

Designed by Ellen Cipriano

Library of Congress Cataloging-in-Publication Data has been applied for.

ISBN: 978-0-06-168432-6

10 11 12 13 14   OV/RRD   10 9 8 7 6 5 4 3 2 1

To my family, thank you for your support, care, and friendship over the years

Contents

THE
1%
WINDFALL

Introduction: The 1% Windfall

There is a fundamental "profit disconnect" in business today. Companies work to bring a product to market by investing significant effort and money in research and development, distribution, and marketing strategies. But when it comes to setting a price—how businesses get compensated for their hard work and financial risk—most companies drop the ball. Critical pricing decisions are often made using arbitrary "this is the way we've always done it" methods. Companies are shortchanging themselves every day.

Most managers aren't comfortable setting prices. With few pricing "golden rules" and little practical guidance for improvement, it's understandable why firms have continued with the status quo. How are companies setting prices today? Most react. Instead of a driver of new profits, prices are a mix of marking up costs, maintaining margins, matching competitors, and seat-of-the-pants analyses.

Since pricing is an underutilized strategy, it is fertile ground for new profits. Focusing on better pricing is a quick path to new profits and growth. Most business improvement initiatives require significant capital investment and long "seed-to-harvest" periods to determine whether or not the effort pays off. In contrast, many of the concepts that I will discuss are straightforward to implement and can start producing profits almost immediately. Consider Costco's signature $1.50 quarter-pound hot dog and soda special. A small increase to $1.52 (and carrying this percentage increase across all of Costco's prices) would boost this warehouse club's operating profits by 48%.[1] And here's the best part: prices can be changed on Sunday night and new profits will start flowing in on Monday morning. I've seen it.

Most companies don't realize the direct link between prices and their profits. It's this connection that makes pricing one of the most powerful strategies available to businesses today. A manufacturing company I work with has operating profits of 5%—it banks 5 cents of every dollar of revenue it collects. If this company raised prices by just 1% (charged, say, $1.01 instead of $1.00), it would earn an extra penny per revenue dollar (its profits would be 6 cents instead of 5 cents). This extra penny translates into a 20% increase in operating profits (1 extra cent per 5 current cents of profit). This calculation, of course, assumes that demand for the product remains constant at the elevated price. The point is that a small change in price can have a big effect on a company's financial bottom line.

A study by McKinsey & Company of the Global 1200 found that if they increased their prices by just 1%, and demand remained constant, on average each company's operating profits would increase by 11%.[2] Based on my analysis of revenue and operating income data from 2008 annual financial statements, Figure I-1 reveals how a 1% price increase would boost the operating incomes of several well-known companies.

Figure I-1 ▥ **1% Windfall for Select Fortune 500 Companies**

THE EFFECTS OF A 1% PRICE INCREASE . . .

Company	1% Windfall Operating Profit Increase
Sears	155%
McKesson	100%
Tyson	81%
Land O'Lakes	58%
Whirlpool	34%
Humana	27%
Amazon	23%
Wal-Mart	18%
Home Depot	16%

*Calculations based on 2008 annual data and assume that demand remains constant after 1% price increase.

The benefits of a 1% price increase are compounded when measured in terms of their effects on a company's market capitalization. The value of a company—how much it is worth—is often calculated as a multiple of its current earnings. The standard convention is to multiply a company's annual earnings by its price-to-earnings ratio (share price divided by net earnings per share) to determine its total value. In the case of Wal-Mart, given its price-to-earnings ratio of 14.56 and 2008 net income of $13.4 billion, an estimate of its market capitalization is $195 billion.[3] Since a 1% price increase leads to a higher net income, this in turn boosts a company's market capitalization. A ballpark measure of the effect of a 1% price increase on Wal-Mart's capitalization involves multiplying the additional net income derived from a 1% price increase ($2.6 billion) by its P/E ratio of 14.56. In this case, Wal-Mart's 1% windfall is roughly an extra $37.9 billion in market capitalization.[4]

These are very powerful results. As I tell my clients, "1% is a small number . . . and achievable."

A PROFIT OPPORTUNITY FOR COMPANIES

Whether the size of a company's 1% windfall is high or low (as measured by operating profit margins, market capitalization, or additional profits), pricing is an important strategy for every business. It is a primary variable in determining profit, as well as a key attribute that consumers consider before making a purchase.

It's surprising how many people within an organization care about and touch prices: CEOs searching for fast profits, CFOs focusing on revenue (instead of cutting costs) to improve financial health, marketing managers setting prices, product managers counting on price to meet their P&L responsibilities, and sales managers seeking new ideas to help with their daily pricing negotiations. Clearly, pricing is an important strategy for many levels of a company.

Without a general philosophy on how to approach pricing issues, it's inevitable that a range of conflicting pricing fiefdoms set up camp within a company. It is common to encounter various managers who want to "keep my margins above a target percentage," "mark up my costs by a fixed amount," or "be the king of market share." Every company has a few who "want to give my customers as many discounts as possible." It's rare to meet a manager focused on using a mix of pricing strategies to make the most profit.

The unavoidable result of these competing pricing philosophies is confusion and frustration. With no means to resolve these differences, it's understandable why many employees end up with an "Oh well . . ." attitude toward pricing. This lackadaisical resignation leads to missed profits and opportunities.

Because of their challenging experiences and the role that pricing plays in their jobs, I've found that staff members are interested in discussing and learning more about pricing. After he read my first pricing book, *The Art of Pricing*, Larry Waxman, president of Waxman Industries, told me: "I like to gather our management team together to discuss our business. Pricing is a good topic that brings my team together—everyone is interested in it. And while I call it a 'pricing meeting,' we always end up talking about other issues too." Pricing is a common denominator throughout a company.

No team can achieve the best results if its members cannot agree on the goals and actions necessary to reach them. Once, while I was moderating a pricing discussion among senior executives of a Fortune 500 company, one participant sat up straight in her chair and said, "Now I finally feel that we are on the same page." And she was right. These executives had a history of bad pricing experiences, and there was an ongoing conflict over how to set prices. Money was being left on the table daily.

This book starts a crucial conversation about pricing that needs to take place within every organization. It creates common ground for better pricing. Most employees take pride in the products and services they provide and want their company to succeed financially. But to do better, they need pricing guidance.

This book helps to solve the universal challenge that every company in the world faces: "What pricing strategy should I create for my products and services?"

IDEAS THAT EVERY COMPANY CAN USE

Having written for academic journals and conducted technical research in a variety of settings, I am well versed in the academic concepts that underpin this book. However, brainstorming in an ivory tower is a long way from helping manufacturers set profitable wholesale prices for Wal-Mart and Wendy's. This book incorporates insights gained from spending the last twenty years working on pricing issues in public policy and the private sector. For most of my career, I've worked directly with companies on their pricing strategies. Today my clients range from a mom-and-pop barbecue restaurant in a small town to multinational companies on Wall Street.

Throughout the book, I will share "success story" interviews that I conducted with managers in a wide variety of industries. These stories showcase the victories of managers who have faced challenging pricing problems. The straightforward pricing strategies they developed and applied have reaped generous windfalls. If these managers can price for profits and growth, you can too.

When I start working with a team of managers on their pricing strategy, it is common for them to caution, "Pricing is unique in our industry." And it's true—most industries have their own pricing nuances. This book highlights and shows techniques to profit from fundamental consumer pricing behaviors that are relevant to all products and services. The ideas and strategies build a foundation to create a pricing strategy for *every* company in the world: any product or service, domestic or international, B2B or B2C, sole proprietors to conglomerates, even nonprofits.

BETTER PRICING IS FAR MORE THAN RAISING PRICES

I've explained the financial benefits of a 1% price increase to illustrate the power of pricing and its direct link to the bottom line. And while companies often have the opportunity to profitably raise prices, I do not advocate a draconian across-the-board price hike. There are other win-win pricing strategies that benefit both companies and their customers. In particular, every company should consider:

- Setting value-based prices
- Activating dormant customers with pick-a-plan
- Using the power of versioning to add product variations
- Offering different prices for the same product

The foundation of better pricing involves setting prices that capture the value that customers place on a product or service. This value-based pricing process begins with identifying what the customer's next-best alternative is and then evaluating its attributes. Value-based pricing uses the next-best alternative's price as a starting point and then adds or subtracts based on product attributes. More bells and whistles command higher prices (an organic fresh turkey versus a frozen Butterball). A stripped-down product yields a lower price (private label versus brand name).

Setting a value-based price involves thinking like a customer when setting prices. Consider the decision process you go through when making a personal purchase. Most of us evaluate a few products and choose the one with the attributes and price that offers the best deal (value) among the various alternatives. It's important to emphasize that the value of a product or service differs by customer and value doesn't necessarily mean the lowest price. After all, many people pay $200 for Dom Pérignon champagne, while others celebrate with $10 Korbel sparkling wine.

Many companies incorrectly set their prices based on what it costs to manufacture a product. The price that consumers are willing to pay depends on the value they place on a product, not how much it costs to make it. Street vendors in Central Park understand this principle. At the first hint of rain, they raise the price of their umbrellas. This increase has nothing to do with costs; instead, it's all about the increased value that customers place on an immediate haven from rain. Better pricing involves capturing value, not marking up costs. Disassociating prices from costs and focusing on capturing value is often a big change for managers. But doing so is fundamental to pricing for profits and growth.

When companies shift to value-based pricing, prices often end up rising. For years, customers may have been smiling and thinking, "I would have paid more." And the truth is, most companies have room to raise some of their prices by 1%. Would an extra 1% (25 cents or so) have caused you to put this book back on the shelf? Companies are usually hesitant to admit that their new pricing strategy resulted in higher prices . . . it isn't exactly endearing to their customers. Cleveland-based industrial manufacturer Parker Hannifin hasn't been shy about acknowledging the benefits of setting prices in a manner that captures the value that customers place on its products.

In 2003, Parker Hannifin abandoned its long-running practice of marking up costs in favor of setting prices based on how customers value its products. "Airlines know they can get away with charging more for a seat to Florida in January than in August. Sports teams raise ticket prices if they're playing a well-known opponent. Why shouldn't Parker do the same?" reasoned CEO Donald Washkewicz.[5]

Viewing pricing through a value-capturing lens, the company discovered that customers were willing to pay more for many of its products. For certain types of metal fittings, Parker Hannifin raised prices between 3% and 60%, with the average increase being 5%. The company claims that the upside of its price changes helped lift net income from $130 million (2002) to $673 million (2006). As a result, Parker Hannifin's shares rose 88% in that time period (compared to a 25% increase in the S&P index).[6]

While increasing prices is tempting and easy to implement, doing so carries some downside risk unless a value-based analysis is used. Consider the 2000 "Return to Love" reunion tour of Diana Ross and members of her former backup group, the Supremes. With tickets priced as high as $250, at some venues there were rows of empty seats. Only 3,000 people attended a Columbus, Ohio, concert in the Value City arena, which holds 22,000, and only 1,400 tickets were sold for the 16,500 seat Hartford XL Center in Connecticut.[7] After twelve of the twenty-three scheduled shows, the tour was cancelled.[8] Commenting on the lackluster sales, concert industry analyst Bob Grossweiner opined: "There has never been a tour bought by a national promoter that's done as bad as this one and had a clash over money like this one."[9] Prices based on the value that customers place on the show would have improved profits and smoothed the path of this less than harmonious reunion tour.

A VALUE-BASED ANALYSIS MAY LEAD TO LOWER PRICES

Setting a value-based price, which I'll discuss further in Chapter 1, some-times leads to a lower price. This strategy may seem counterintuitive, as lower prices result in thinner margins. However, a lower price can actu-ally result in higher profits because more customers say, "I'll buy." These new customers compensate for the resulting slimmer margins.

The summer 2005 "employee pricing" blowout sale by the Big Three automakers (Ford, GM, and Chrysler) illustrates the benefits of lowering price. Approaching a new model year with unprecedented inventory levels, another ordinary summer sale wasn't going to clear the lots. To demonstrate its commitment to offering its best prices, General Motors took the revolutionary step of offering to the public the prices that its employees pay for vehicles. Ford and Chrysler followed with similar plans. The concept of "employee pricing" resonated with consumers—everyone appreciates getting an insider deal. In its first month, Ford's sales rose by 29%, Chrysler's went up by 32%, and GM tallied a 41% sales increase, making it the third best sales month in history.[10]

PICK-A-PLAN: ROLL OUT NEW PRICING PLANS

Customers are often interested in a product but refrain from purchasing because the selling strategy does not work for them. While some want to purchase outright, others may prefer another pricing plan such as rent, lease, prepay, or all-you-can-eat (or use). A pick-a-plan strategy ac-tivates these dormant customers. Pick-a-plan is the concept of offering a pricing plan that generates growth by better understanding and better serving customers. Providing a pricing plan that satisfies a key need of an underserved segment can generate big growth.

Some companies base their entire business strategy on a new

pricing plan. A great illustration of the power of pick-a-plan pricing involves my friend Fred Straus. For his seventieth birthday, Fred decided to splurge on a weeklong Caribbean vacation with his wife, children, and grandchildren. Inquiring about his destination, he emphasized: "I *have* to go to an all-inclusive resort—it would kill me to see my grandchildren on the beach drinking $5 Coca-Colas all day." What a fascinating response . . . and a pricing concern that most of us can relate to. It's interesting that, of all the attributes available when booking a Caribbean vacation (island, hotel characteristics, local activities, price, and so on), an all-inclusive price was at the top of Fred's list. By offering an all-inclusive plan, resorts satisfy an important need of customers like Fred who value and are willing to pay a premium for the freedom of not having to think about the price of every meal, drink, or activity while on vacation. Offering this pricing option moves a resort to the top of the list for these vacationers.

DIFFERENTIAL PRICING: OFFER LOWER PRICES

The law of demand, as illustrated by a downward-sloping demand curve, offers a key pricing principle: some customers are willing to pay more than others. Differential pricing is the strategy of selling the same product to different customers at different prices.

Customers are often interested in a product but hold off purchasing because it is too expensive. The drawback of lowering prices to attract these price-sensitive customers is that profit is lost from those who are willing to pay the current higher price. One option to minimize this loss is to offer targeted discounts. This strategy can be accomplished by creating a hurdle that customers must jump over to receive a discount. The notion is that only price-sensitive customers will jump over the hurdle to snare the discount. Customers who don't make this effort (less price-sensitive customers) will continue to pay current prices.

An example of a hurdle discount strategy is the TKTS theater ticket booths in London and New York. On the day of the performance, many theaters sell their excess inventory through these TKTS booths at 25% to 50% off. Value-conscious consumers line up daily in hopes of getting a good deal on a theatrical experience.

This strategy does a good job of segmenting discount-oriented from full-paying customers. Suppose that you are vacationing in London and seeing *The Phantom of the Opera* in the famed West End theater district would be a trip highlight. Would you forgo purchasing full-price tickets in advance to wait in line in hopes that tickets (and perhaps good seats) are available? Probably not. Those who want to see a specific play (higher-valuation customers) pay full price, while those who care less which play they see (lower-valuation customers) queue up for a discount.

VERSIONING: ADD PRODUCT VARIATIONS

While it's possible to offer a handful of differential prices, it's not realistic to set a unique price for every customer interested in a product. The popular strategy of versioning involves using a core product as a base and adding/subtracting attributes in a manner that appeals to more customers.

A common versioning tactic involves offering good, better, and best product versions. Those who highly value a product purchase the best version, while customers with lower valuations select the good or better products. In summer 2007, Scholastic released regular ($34.99) and deluxe ($65.00) versions of the final book in the Harry Potter series, *Harry Potter and the Deathly Hallows*. On the first day of their presale, the regular and deluxe editions were respectively the number one and number two best-selling books on both Amazon, as well as the Barnes and Noble websites.[11]

Fast-food chains have used discount versions of their signature products to cater to lower-valuation customers. Instead of paying $3.79

for a Big Mac, value-conscious buyers can dine on a comparable $1 McDouble cheeseburger at McDonald's. Burger King claims that 13% of its revenues come from its value menu products, while both Wendy's and McDonald's confirm that "well over 20%" of their revenues come from their lower-priced versions.[12] While offering low margins, good versions promote growth by selling to price-sensitive customers who might not otherwise purchase. Best versions provide higher profits from capturing the premium value that some customers place on a product.

Versioning can also involve adding attributes to a product that customers value, which leads to serving new segments. Caffeine-free versions of beverages, for instance, generate growth by opening those products to new consumers.

A PRICING WINDFALL FOR SOUTHWEST AIRLINES

A hallmark of better pricing is the ease with which it can be developed and implemented. Consider the pricing windfall created by Southwest Airlines. In the summer of 2007, the mood in the Dallas boardroom was tense. With rising fuel prices and a weakening economy, Southwest Airlines was facing one of the toughest market environments in its history. CEO Gary C. Kelly was clear in his directive: declining revenues were not acceptable. Kevin Krone, a vice president of marketing, sales, and distribution, was tasked to "create a reason for people to give us more money."[13] Yet there was one key constraint. A fundamental component of Southwest's brand is its role as an ally of the customer. Price increases had to be kept to a minimum.

"It was one of the biggest challenges of my career," Kevin confided.[14] He was looking for a "win for the customer, win for the company" strategy with the potential to score a dramatic success. One area that he focused on was Southwest's desire to enhance its product for business travelers.

A great part of Southwest's success is its remarkable twenty-five-minute turnaround time for unloading incoming passengers, cleaning the aircraft, and loading outbound passengers. An important component of this efficiency is Southwest's "first come, first served" boarding policy. Based on when they arrive at the airport (or when they checked in on the website), passengers are allocated A, B, and C boarding passes that determine the order of boarding the plane. The A passes are the most desirable because they allow passengers to board first and get the best pick of seats.

Over the years, many passengers had let Southwest know that they were willing to pay extra for a guaranteed A pass. This makes sense; how much would you pay to avoid sitting in a middle seat on a cross-country flight? To meet these customer needs, Kevin and his team created a new airline ticket category, which they labeled Business Select. For $10–$30 more than the airline's highest fares, a Business Select ticket provides a guaranteed A pass, enhanced frequent-flyer credit, and an alcoholic beverage. "Why an alcoholic beverage?" I asked Kevin. In his research, he told me, he'd found that many business passengers think of a cocktail as a "reward to cap the day."

Business Select has been a success. Just a few months after rolling out this new fare type, Southwest was selling two or three of these enhanced tickets per flight. The program was on track to generate an incremental $100 million in new revenue in its first year.[15] While Southwest's exact profit figures are confidential, my back-of-the-envelope calculations hint that this new ticket could reap as much as $80 million in additional operating profits. This represents over 10% of Southwest's 2007 operating profit. What's best about this pricing innovation is that Southwest benefits, of course, but its customers are also better off. Interestingly, the majority of travelers purchasing Business Select tickets are its current customers. They voluntarily elected to pay Southwest more money for a feature they value. Customer compliments on this new Business Select ticket include "All I have to say to Southwest is thank you, thank you, thank you!" "Thanks for the superb service," and "I am so happy with the new boarding process."[16]

This kind of pricing innovation keeps Southwest a profit leader in the airline industry. As we were ending our interview, I asked Kevin what lessons he learned about pricing during this experience. He confidently responded, "Customers are different . . . they have different needs and desires."

Kevin's conclusions illustrate an important theme of this book: creating a pricing strategy involves acknowledging, serving, and profiting from the fact that customers are different in terms of their pricing needs.

PRICING IS INTEGRAL TO ACHIEVING SUCCESS

The definition of success often differs by company. Key success metrics include (1) market share, (2) operating margin targets, and (3) profitable growth (boosting a primary financial barometer, such as operating profits, by a target percentage). Regardless of which metric a company measures itself by, pricing plays an important role in meeting its goals.

1. *Market share.* If maximizing market share is the goal, traditional thinking is that lower prices lead to more purchases (and higher market share). This old-school perspective often leads companies to adopt a "how low can I go" pricing mentality. Contrary to this long-held belief, the pricing techniques in this book empower companies to both maximize market share and earn the highest profits. I'll return to this concept in Chapter 7.

2. *Operating margin targets.* Improving operating margins is often viewed as a sign of a company's vitality. The two primary methods to improve operating margins are cost reduction and better pricing. In Chapter 7, I discuss why operating margins are not the best measure of success.

3. *Profitable growth.* This involves setting quarterly or annual targets on a key metric such as operating profit growth rates.

Achieving this goal involves cost control, pricing actions, and volume growth (which is often influenced by price).

Pricing is also important for nonprofits to reach their goal of serving a large constituency. Higher margins can be used to improve services as well as subsidize those with lower incomes.

The pricing concepts and strategies in this book are relevant to achieving all of these success metrics. Capturing value and using pricing strategies to serve target customer segments are the right pricing philosophies for every company to rally around. Additionally, since most companies don't fully incorporate value into their prices, adopting this practice provides a distinct competitive advantage.

BETTER PRICING AND CUSTOMER FAIRNESS

Sometimes when I work with a team of executives on their company's pricing strategy, I sense an uneasiness with the goal of pricing for profits and growth. This hesitancy is understandable, given that better pricing has traditionally been thought of as raising prices: "It's time for our annual 4% price increase." Boosting prices in this manner—a company's gain comes directly from consumers' wallets—brings up fears of being accused of taking advantage of customers.

It's important to discuss these concerns and resolve any ambivalence about pricing for profits and growth. First, as I have already alluded to, the majority of the pricing strategies that I discuss involve discounting prices, offering consumers choices of lower- or higher-priced product versions, and better serving customer needs with new pricing plans and product versions. Just as the results of the Business Select ticket version benefited both Southwest and its customers, these are good for the customer *and* good for company pricing strategies.

A commonly held belief is that setting a low price creates goodwill with customers. Yes, most consumers appreciate a low price. The problem is that many sellers believe this goodwill ensures that customers will continue purchasing even if a better value on a competitor's product becomes available. That's not the case. If a similar or higher-quality product with a lower price enters the market, how many customers will continue purchasing an inferior and higher-priced product? Instead of lowering prices, I suggest less costly efforts such as a friendly greeting or providing extraordinary service to engender goodwill.

When better pricing initiatives result in a higher price, is this unethical or unfair? Not necessarily. Companies are entitled to profit from the value and usefulness of the products that they create. Many people invest their time and money to bring a product to market. They have taken financial and career risks and are entitled to profit from the value of their products. And remember, if a product fails, customers aren't going to purchase out of fairness or ethics.

While capturing value may result in a price increase, it is important to emphasize that the primary goal of the strategies offered in this book is to serve as many customers as possible. How is this possible with a higher price? As you will see, my pricing philosophy is that offering "back-door" discounts such as off-peak prices, coupons, and end-of-the season sales to price-sensitive customers, as well as enticing customers with new versions and pricing plans, is just as important as setting a value-based price.

Finally, don't forget the benefits that customers receive when they make a transaction. When a customer decides to purchase, he or she is in essence saying, "Thank you, I considered all of the competing products and decided that yours offers me the best value."

PRICING FOR PROFITS AND GROWTH OVERVIEW

Today, pricing is generally viewed as a two-lever strategy: raise or lower prices. As I have stated and will continue to demonstrate, there are a myriad of pricing tactics available, each one capable of delivering a pricing windfall. And while many of the tactics may seem incremental, remember, we are only looking for 1%. One stylistic point to note: I will be discussing pricing strategies for products. By *products*, I mean any product or service.

Figure I-2 ■ Key Terms

PRODUCT:

  any product or service.

COMPANY (BUSINESS):

  refers to any company (small or big, domestic or multinational). Many of the concepts also apply to nonprofit organizations as well as government agencies.

This book is divided into three sections. Part I focuses in greater detail on value-based pricing, the foundation of better pricing. This section offers two ways to calculate a value-based price for products. Part II discusses the strategy of pricing. These chapters discuss three pricing nuances that companies can capitalize on. Chapter 2 highlights that some customers prefer different pricing plans. To serve these customers, companies should offer a variety of pick-a-plan tactics. Chapter 3 centers on how different customers have different product needs. As a result, small changes to products can create new opportunities to profit and grow. Good, better, and best versions also target customers with a wide range of product valuations. Chapter 4 focuses on the truism that some customers are willing to pay more than others for the same product. To profit from these variations, companies can charge different prices to different customers.

With these fundamental principles and associated strategies established, the key challenge becomes: "How do I use these insights and tactics to create my own company's pricing strategy?" This is the focus of Part III. Chapter 5 provides frameworks and strategy templates to set an offensive pricing strategy. Chapter 6 shows how the pricing concepts and strategies can be used in defensive pricing situations including recession, inflation, and price wars. Of course, understanding how to set prices is important, but it is necessary to have a company-wide environment that encourages pricing for profits and growth. To address this, Chapter 7 focuses on principles that can create a culture of profit, which aligns and supports employees in their better pricing efforts. Finally, Chapter 8 presents an action plan that shows how to roll out the frameworks, concepts, strategies, tactics, and principles of a comprehensive pricing strategy.

KEY TAKEAWAYS

THE 1% WINDFALL

- Better pricing is not difficult to understand and implement. This book provides a set of actionable frameworks to allow companies to use price to profit and grow.
- To illustrate the power of better pricing, calculate your company's potential 1% windfall by answering the following question: "How would a 1% increase in price affect operating profits?"
- It's easy to calculate a 1% pricing windfall by using revenue and operating profit data from a company's financial statement. Suppose a product has revenues of $100 and clears $5 in operating profits. Assuming demand doesn't change, a 1% increase in price would lead to $101 in revenues and $6 of operating profits. Thus, a 1% increase in price would generate a 20% increase in operating profits.
- Regardless of the size of a company's 1% windfall, pricing is a crucial strategy for every business. It is a primary variable in determining profit as well as a key attribute that consumers consider before making a purchase.
- No matter what product or service a company offers, every company in the world can benefit from better pricing: domestic or

international, B2B or B2C, sole proprietors or conglomerates, even nonprofits.

- Many people in a given organization are interested in, affected by, and touch pricing, including CEOs, CFOs, product managers, marketing managers, and the sales force.
- Regardless of the metric of success used to evaluate a company (market share, operating margins, profitable growth), value-based pricing is essential to achieving success.
- Value-based pricing, deriving prices by considering how customers make purchasing decisions, involves setting prices that capture the value customers place on a product.
- Most of the pricing strategies in this book are win-win for both buyers and sellers. Lowering prices and offering targeted discounts allow new customers to enjoy a product as well. Similarly, offering different pricing plans and versions gives consumers a chance to select what works best for them.
- Better pricing is powerful and easy to implement, quickly produces results, and focuses a company on creating and capturing new value.

PART ONE

The Foundation of Pricing: Value-Based Pricing

The first part of this book is composed of Chapter 1 only. This is a critical chapter that introduces value-based pricing, which is the foundation of pricing for profits and growth.

Thinking about and setting prices based on a product's value is a new concept for most companies. And while change is often a challenge, the commonsense reasoning in this chapter demonstrates why value-based pricing should be adopted for all products.

One of the most important takeaway messages of this book is: *set prices to capture a product's value.*

1

Capture Value by Thinking Like a Customer

By setting prices to capture the value that a product provides relative to the next-best alternatives, Olivier Biebuyck and his colleagues took a waste product that many considered to be valueless and earned millions of dollars of new profits for Lafarge North America, the Fortune Global 500 building materials company.

Olivier is a driven executive who is always focused on profit: if there is money to be made, he will find it. Booking new profits is exactly what he started searching for on his first day as vice president of cementitious materials at Lafarge's corporate headquarters in Herndon, Virginia. This new job was politically tricky. In the past, most key operating decisions involving cementitious materials were made at one of Lafarge's twenty district outposts, which oversee more than a thousand locations in the United States and Canada. But now many of these decisions were being recentralized to Olivier. "I needed to build credibility quickly," he shared with me.[1] As he reviewed stacks of status reports, he honed in on pricing. In particular, he couldn't understand why the fly ash prices were all over the map.

Fly ash is the residue generated from coal-fired power plants. It is usually dumped in landfills as waste. As it turns out, fly ash can be used as an ingredient to make concrete.[2] Replacing some cement (which is an expensive component of concrete) with fly ash can result in stronger concrete with a smoother finish. Fly ash can replace 15–20% of cement in a concrete mixture depending on the type of application, such as pavement, walls, and patios. Lafarge's role as a middleman between power plants and concrete manufacturers involves the company in distribution, quality control, marketing, and technical research about fly ash's benefits.

A key issue for fly ash is its poor image: concrete manufacturers viewed it as a waste product . . . which it is. Some even suggested that they should be paid to take fly ash, since it saves on landfill disposal costs for utility companies. With little being done to battle this perception, prices were at rock bottom, barely covering distribution and storage costs.

With no clear story about how prices were being set, Olivier started inviting himself to meetings. "Let's discuss pricing," he'd suggest. Up to this point, the sales force had had wide discretion in setting fly ash prices. With little guidance on setting prices from headquarters and a limited understanding of the potential upside from better pricing, fly ash prices weren't a pressing issue for the organization. Undeterred, Olivier focused on setting prices by thinking from his customers' point of view: "What's the next-best alternative that concrete producers have to fly ash? Buying expensive cement that produces lower-quality concrete. Let's educate our customers about the benefits of fly ash," he encouraged at meetings. "It's lower-cost, it produces quality results, and it's ecologically green."

The renewed sales efforts from district managers and the focus on the benefits of fly ash particularly helped Lafarge's customers during the high-demand summer months, when cement was in short supply. Instead of facing costly construction delays while they wait for cement, concrete customers now mix in fly ash instead.

While some concrete producers balked, even with the price hike, fly ash was a great deal compared to its next-best alternative. Two-and-a-half years later, in great part due to his team's focus on setting prices that capture value, Olivier's division's operating profits have doubled.

What's your company's fly ash?

VALUE-BASED PRICE: THE FOUNDATION OF BETTER PRICING

For many companies, thinking like their customers and setting prices that capture value are fundamental shifts in the way they create their pricing strategy. Most don't focus on capturing value today. Instead, they mark up their cost ("I set prices by doubling costs") or focus on margins ("I need a 30% margin over costs"). While it's easy to set prices this way (just a few calculator keystrokes), money is left on the table. A price that's based on cost bears no relation to what customers might pay. When you are shopping, do you deem a price acceptable if it is double the cost to produce the item or is 30% higher than the item's cost? Instead we consider several alternatives presented to us on a store shelf or in a showroom and choose the one that's best for us.

The key to better pricing is to set value-based prices. As New York City street vendors Parker Hannifin and Olivier Biebuyck have demonstrated, this simple change in how a company thinks about pricing alone can reap a windfall.

There are two primary approaches to setting value-based prices. A *one-on-one price* is used when setting (or negotiating) a price to sell one unit of a product to a single customer. A *multicustomer price* is used when setting a unit price to sell many units of a product to more than one customer.

Why two pricing methodologies? Setting a price to sell multiple products to different customers requires more analysis (which involves constructing a demand curve) compared to calculating a price meant for a single consumer. We'll start off with the basics of one-on-one pricing, and then build on those principles to create a multicustomer demand curve.

Figure 1-1 ■ What Pricing Methodology Should Be Used?

Pricing Methodology	Applicability
One-on-one	Selling one product (or service) to one customer (home, used car, negotiating a custom service).
Multicustomer	Selling many units of a product to a variety of customers. Most products and services are in this category.

METHODOLOGY 1: ONE-ON-ONE PRICING

Here's a simple example that illustrates the key principles of setting a value-based price. Suppose you own a beach house that you rent to vacationers by the week. The house next door is also available for rent. The only difference: yours has a swimming pool. Everything else is identical. A potential renter is deciding which house to use for summer vacation. What is the highest weekly rental price at which you can close the deal right now?

Step 1: Identify target customers. Vacationers looking to rent a beach house for a week.

Step 2: Identify their next-best alternative. The beach house next door. Use this product's price as a starting point.

Step 3: Determine your product's difference. In this case, your house has a pool.

Step 4: Calculate your product's value based on its differentiation. Suppose from your experienced judgment you've determined the average vacationer will pay a 20% premium over their next-best alternative for a pool.

Step 5: Do a reality check. Before basing your price on your customer's next-best alternative, you have to undertake two analyses. First, determine if the base price is realistic. If the price of the next-best alternative is too high (customers aren't willing to pay it), it's not a valid price to use as a starting point. Second, ask yourself, "Can I make money at this price? Does the price at least cover variable costs?"

Suppose your neighbor sets an unrealistically high price of $2,000 per week (when, according to online classified ads for similar houses, the price should be $1,000 per week). If you simply add a 20% pool premium to calculate your price ($2,400 per week), both houses will sit vacant.

There are three potential outcomes of this reality check:

Your neighbor's $1,000 price is reasonable. Set your price at
   $1,200 ($1,000 + 20%).
Your neighbor's $2,000 price is too high. Use experienced
   judgment and/or ancillary data to determine a reasonable
   base price ($1,000). Thus, your price should be $1,200
   ($1,000 + 20%).
Your neighbor's $500 price is too low. As many e-tailers learned
   during the Internet boom, this low price has to be used as
   the base because this highly discounted price is a viable
   option for consumers. One point to keep in mind: when
   customers get a good deal, they may be willing to pay a
   more generous premium for higher-quality attributes (called
   an *income effect*): "Since I can get a great deal on a house
   without a pool, I'm now willing to pay 30% more for a pool."[3]
   If this is the case, your price should be $650 ($500 + 30%).

Step 4 in this process is critical. Why is the pool premium 20%? How about 15% or 25%? To determine the value of a pool, you have to think like your customers. After all, it's their personal judgment that determines the price they will pay. Because of this, there's no simple

Figure 1-2

FIVE STEPS TO A
ONE-ON-ONE VALUE-BASED PRICE

STEP 1	STEP 2	STEP 3	STEP 4	STEP 5
Identify target customers	Determine their next best alternative	Understand how the product differs	Calculate value based on differentiation	Do a reality check

formula that can calculate a value-based price. Consumer insights on value can be gleaned through two primary methods: experienced judgment or market research methods. Companies often rely on experienced judgment supported by insights from existing market research. In this case, the 20% premium could have been derived from years of beach house rental experience or a recent conversation with a local realtor.

What role, if any, do costs play in setting a value-based price? They set boundaries. Of course, to make a profit, on average prices have to be greater than total costs. While prime holiday weeks will garner top dollar, at other times prices need to be discounted to accommodate reduced customer value. What's the lowest price you can set during off-peak periods, such as those first two weeks of August, when jellyfish invade the beach? Suppose your mortgage (divided by fifty-two weeks) is $450 a week and the additional cost of renting is $300 per week (commission to agent, cleaning fees). In other words, you have $450 of fixed costs (incurred regardless of whether the house is rented or not) and $300 of variable costs (incurred only if the house is rented) per week. During low customer valuation weeks, any price above variable costs ($300) is acceptable because it contributes to fixed overhead that will be incurred anyway.

Admittedly, there are a limited number of one-on-one pricing situations. Examples include selling a house, selling a used car, or setting a custom job price for one customer. This methodology can also be used for business-to-business transactions, such as a faucet manufacturer, to highlight their product's value. When pitching a major retailer such as Lowe's to start carrying its product, a manufacturer needs to convey why consumers prefer its product over those currently on the retailer's shelves. Demonstrating that a product offers a trusted brand, improved features, or generous warranty that customers are willing to pay a premium for are valued-based arguments that can convince retailers to stock a new product.

Most important, this methodology illustrates the fundamental points of pricing that are relevant to every pricing situation (regardless of the number of products being sold or customers). First, value-based prices are based on a product's next-best alternative. This is why movie theaters charge more for refreshments than supermarkets (few alternatives versus many alternatives). Second, and just as important, value-based pricing focuses on capturing the value customers place on how a product differs from its next-best alternative. If a product offers premium attributes, there's room to set higher prices. Conversely, fewer attributes (stripped-down products) necessitate a discount.

Figure 1-3
SUMMARY OF KEY
VALUE-BASED PRICING POINTS

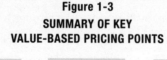

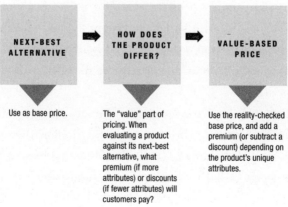

NEXT-BEST ALTERNATIVE	HOW DOES THE PRODUCT DIFFER?	VALUE-BASED PRICE
Use as base price.	The "value" part of pricing. When evaluating a product against its next-best alternative, what premium (if more attributes) or discounts (if fewer attributes) will customers pay?	Use the reality-checked base price, and add a premium (or subtract a discount) depending on the product's unique attributes.

HOW DOES A PRODUCT DIFFER FROM
ITS NEXT-BEST ALTERNATIVE?

A product's price should be based on the next-best alternative's price simply because it's a viable option. If Pepsi's price is too high, some customers—those for whom the drinks are interchangeable—will buy Coke, and vice versa. If a product is perceived as similar to the competition's, it has to charge the same (or lower) price as the rival. After all, why would customers pay more for an identical product? The opportunity to charge a different price comes from understanding the value that customers place on a product's unique characteristics relative to its competitors. Key characteristics that differentiate a product might include brand, quality, attributes, service, ease of purchase, and style.

Brand. A pledge of satisfaction and quality. A well-known brand conveys trust, quality, and/or style. Luxury retailer Tiffany has built a reputation of offering "the best." This message is conveyed via its signature blue gift box. Investigating how much of a premium the Tiffany brand can command, ABC News consumer reporter Elisabeth Leamy purchased a nearly flawless diamond slightly over a carat with a unique Tiffany setting for $16,600. Independent appraisers valued this diamond, without the Tiffany setting, at roughly $10,000. Shopping at the other end of the brand spectrum, the reporter also purchased a diamond with similar specs at Costco for $6,600 without a setting. Master gemologist Martin Fuller, who appraised both diamonds, commented: "It's a little bit of a surprise. You wouldn't normally consider a fine diamond to be found in a general store like Costco, but I'm pleasantly surprised."[4]

Quality. A higher degree of excellence than the norm. If a product offers better quality, charge for it. Jamón Ibérico de Bellota is considered by many to be the finest-tasting ham in the world. Made from pigs raised in southern Spain and prized for their well-marbled meat, it is currently selling for $179.99 a pound . . . a bit more expensive than the $14.99 a pound for its very distant cousin, Jamón Serrano ham.[5]

Attributes. Physical characteristics of a product. These are key physical features that distinguish products, such as size, power, and capabilities. Because cable Internet has almost double the connection speed compared to the high-speed DSL service offered by telephone companies, its services are generally priced higher.

Service. Ancillary nonphysical characteristics of a product fall under the category of service. Premium retailer Nordstrom is well known for the lengths its sales representatives go to in order to provide great service. Most famous is the story of the returned tires. A customer went to the Fairbanks, Alaska, Nordstrom store with two tires, receipt in hand, and demanded a refund. Even though Nordstrom doesn't sell tires, the clerk accepted the return and refunded the purchase. Why? Nordstrom had bought out a dry goods company, previously located at the same address, that sold tires. That's great customer service.[6]

Ease of purchase. Level of convenience involved in locating and purchasing a product. The more effort it takes to make a purchase, the lower the value. As a result, a product's value decreases if its distribution is not plentiful (customers have to drive sixty miles to purchase it or wait to receive it by mail) or its retailers don't take credit cards. Similarly, banks with more ATMs offer higher value than those with fewer locations.

Style. The distinctive artistic expression of a product is its style. One attribute that customers appreciate about Apple's products is their sleek design. An eye-catching style or unique color can often entice customers to say, "I'll buy."

These characteristics differentiate a given product from its next-best alternative and thus allow a different price to be charged. I'm often surprised when companies set their prices by matching a competitor's price. Pointing out these matching prices, I ask, "You mean your product is exactly the same as your competitor's?" "Of course not—ours is better," company employees reply. If your product is better than your competitor's offering, tell your customers. Scream it, point to it, brag about it . . . then set prices that capture the value consumers place on your product's uniqueness.

VALUE REVISITED: DIFFERENT CUSTOMERS
MEAN DIFFERENT VALUATIONS

The challenge of setting a price is that every customer values a product's unique characteristics differently. This translates into a different willingness to pay. Some customers (families) are willing to pay more than others (sightseers) for a pool at their rental beach house. Some prefer Prada, while others don't. The root of these differences lies in the way in which customers subjectively and objectively determine value.

Subjective value. Derived from personal taste, subjective value is generally the most important determinant of willingness to pay. Since taste is in the eye of the beholder, subjective value varies significantly from consumer to consumer. No formula can decipher why one man wears blue ties while another prefers yellow ones. This heterogeneity in taste is also apparent in furniture style choices. Many people take pride in their French country antiques, whereas some are into art deco, and others are comfortable with shabby chic. Personal taste is a key reason why customers have different valuations for products and services.

Objective value. Usually more quantifiable, objective value reflects a more understandable rationale for some customers to prefer one product over another. Homeowners with large yards generally place a higher valuation on John Deere riding mowers relative to those with smaller lawns. Similarly, more expensive Energy Star–certified fluorescent lightbulbs last up to ten times longer and are more energy-efficient compared to regular lightbulbs. So why doesn't everyone buy these bulbs? Some opt not to purchase because they don't use their lamps as much as others. This lower usage results in a longer payback period for the up-front premium, making it not as worthwhile for some. Objective value illustrates that some customers demonstrably benefit from—and thus value—a product more than others.

Auctions illustrate that customers have different valuations. When bidding for an item starts, many potential buyers eagerly participate. But as the price creeps up, buyers waver. When a bidder drops out, he or she is in effect saying: "I see that others are still bidding, but the price has reached a point where it's not worth it to me anymore." Check out the bidding history of any eBay completed auction, and you'll see the various price points when bidders declared, "The price has become too expensive for me."

How much would you pay to have lunch with billionaire investor Warren Buffett? Every year the Glide Foundation (a nonprofit San Francisco group that helps the poor and homeless) auctions off the opportunity to lunch with Warren Buffett. During this three-hour meeting, the winner can discuss whatever he or she wants with this investment legend except for his thoughts on specific stocks. In June 2009, the bidding for this opportunity started at $25,000. Five days and 116 bids later, the steak lunch with Buffett sold for $1.68 million dollars to Salida Capital, a Toronto hedge fund. This amount was lower than the $2.11 million winning bid in 2008 for a similar luncheon.[7] Commenting on the purchase, Salida Capital CEO Courtenay Wolfe said, "We are happy to get it for the price that we got it for. Particularly going through such sensitive times, his [Buffett's] wisdom and experience is of great value to us, and we believe it's an investment in our future."[8]

Customers are unique in their subjective and objective valuations of a product. Because of these differences, for any given product, some customers are willing to pay more than others. This concept is critical to setting a value-based price for a product that is sold to more than one customer.

METHODOLOGY 2: MULTICUSTOMER PRICING

In the beach house example, the goal was to rent a quantity of one (a week's rental) to one customer. Realistically though, most businesses sell more than one unit of their product to a variety of customers. In this multicustomer selling situation, setting a value-based price involves analyzing the trade-off between price and quantity sold. A discount price attracts more customers who have lower valuations, and it also encourages repeat purchases. This leads to more goods sold. However, the downside of a lower price is that it reduces the margin per product sold. The challenge of a multicustomer pricing analysis is to find the price that is the most profitable given this trade-off between margin and products sold.

Figure 1-4
FOUR STEPS TO A MULTICUSTOMER
VALUE-BASED PRICE

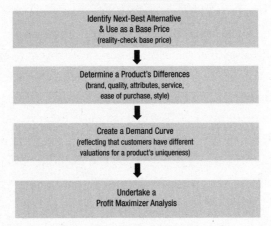

To find this "right" price, begin the same way as in the one-on-one analysis: identify target customers and their next-best alternative, and understand your product's differentiating characteristics. What's new is the need to incorporate the concept of different customer valuations for a product's unique characteristics into the analysis.

Consider two desktop computers that are identical in every aspect except for the warranty. One offers a three-year warranty that involves sending the computer back to the manufacturer and then waiting for it to be returned after being repaired. This is a laborious and time-consuming process. The other provides a more convenient and time-saving three-year warranty that offers next-day repair service at your home or office. Of course, if these desktop computers were identical in every respect (including warranty), their prices also would have to be the same; there would be no reason to pay more. However, since one offers a better warranty, there is an opportunity to raise its price relative to the rival's. How much more should be charged? Since many desktops are being sold, the analysis has to take into account that some computer owners value this enhanced warranty more than others. A few may pay a $350 premium for the warranty, while more will pay $100. To determine the "right" price, the one that generates the most profit, requires constructing a demand curve.

Creating a demand curve like those that you may have studied in Economics 101 may seem difficult. But trust me: you don't need a Ph.D. to create one.

Figure 1-5
DOWNWARD SLOPING DEMAND CURVE

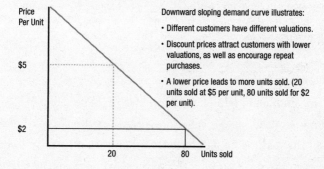

A company spokesperson asks first, "Whoever will pay $5 for the product, raise your hand," and then counts the relatively small number of hands in the air. The next question would be: "Now, whoever will pay $4 for this product, raise your hand." There will be more hands this time. Everyone who would have paid $5 will certainly pay $4, and some people who will pay between $4 and $5 will be added to the group.

Example: Understanding a Demand Curve

Suppose a company has assembled all of its customers together in a parking lot. These customers have agreed to be honest and reveal the true value (highest price) they place on a product. The highest price that any customer will pay is $5 and the lowest is $1.

A company spokesperson asks first, "Whoever will pay $5 for the product, raise your hand," and then counts the relatively small number of hands in the air. The next question would be: "Now, whoever will pay $4 for this product, raise your hand." There will be more hands this time. Everyone who would have paid $5 will certainly pay $4, and some people who will pay between $4 and $5 will be added to the group.

PRICE ELASTICITY

Chances are that you have heard the term *elasticity* used in pricing. And for that reason, it's an important term to understand even though it isn't an integral component of setting the most profitable price. Elasticity answers the question, "If price is changed, what will happen to revenue?"
A price point is considered:

Elastic if lowering price results in higher revenue and increasing price reduces revenue
Unit elastic if changing price (increase or decrease) results in unchanged revenue
Inelastic if lowering price decreases revenue and increasing price generates higher revenue

Elasticity only focuses on revenues, not profits. While it's nice to know how revenues will be affected by changing price, most of us are more interested in what will happen to profits as price changes. This metric is the focus of a profit maximizer analysis.

Count this number of hands. The response to "Who will pay $3?" leads to even more raised hands. When the price level finally reaches $1, everyone in the parking lot will have their hands in the air. A lower price attracts customers in two ways. First, those who previously raised their hands at higher prices will certainly purchase at a lower one. Second, a discounted price attracts new customers.

Counting the total number of raised hands at each price level (a few at $5, more at $3, and all at $1) yields the data necessary to create a demand curve. Graphically, the downward slope of a demand curve exhibits this trade-off between price and sales.

One point to note about demand curves is that in general, no matter what price is set, some customers would have paid more. Consider a $4 price: customers who raised their hands at $4, as well as those who had their hands in the air at $5 will buy. The $5 customers are musing, "I would have paid $1 more," while $4 customers are thinking, "The price is exactly right. Anything higher and I would not have bought."

Profit-Maximizer Analysis

Once a demand curve is constructed, the next task is to determine the right price. A high price yields large margins but minimal sales. A low price generates more sales but thinner margins. Companies are looking for the price that makes the most money from this trade-off between profit per product and quantity sold.

Looking at a demand curve and wondering what price will generate the largest profits can be intimidating. However, undertaking what I call a *profit maximizer analysis* is straightforward to complete. The crux of a profit maximizer analysis is asking and answering the following question: "How much profit will be made at key price levels?"

A profit maximizer analysis involves first determining revenues, costs, and profits at different price levels. After these data are available, the next step is to select the price associated with the highest profits.

Figure 1-6
PROFIT MAXIMIZER ANALYSIS

	PRICE PER UNIT	UNITS SOLD	TOTAL REVENUE	TOTAL COSTS	PROFITS	
Start at $5 and proceed downwards	$5	20	$100	$40	$60	
	$4	40	$160	$80	$80	✓ Set the price that yields the highest profit
	$3	60	$180	$120	$60	
	$2	80	$160	$160	$0	
	$1	100	$100	$200	($100)	

Cost = $2 per unit manufactured

Constructing a Demand Curve

Since most companies set a single price to sell more than one unit of product to a variety of customers, they have to create a demand curve. This curve can be created by using market research, experienced judgment, or one-on-one pricing methodology (in cases when money, data, and experienced judgment are low or time is of the essence).

Market research. Conjoint analysis, an advanced market research technique, can be used to create a demand curve. By surveying how customers choose products in various pricing scenarios, insights can be gained about their willingness to pay for a product, as well as how much they value key attributes. Because of its cost and the relatively long time needed to undertake the research, few companies use this market research technique to estimate demand. A more detailed discussion is beyond the scope of this book, but information about conjoint analysis is widely available.[9]

Experienced judgment. A demand curve estimate can be generated by using existing data and experience that a company has on hand. Companies may have hard data on several price points, such as quantity sold at the current price, as well as how demand changed due to recent discount sale prices. Experienced judgment (from the sales force and representatives who observe customer reactions to price every day) can be used to fill in a demand curve.

One-on-one pricing. There are many times when pricing data are inadequate and there is only limited experienced judgment to go by (common with new-to-the-world products that customers have yet to evaluate), or perhaps a company isn't in a position to undertake market research. In these situations, one option is to revert back to the one-on-one pricing methodology and evaluate how the *average* customer values a product. To ensure profitability, this one-on-one price must be higher than the product's average cost.

Obviously, experienced judgment and one-on-one pricing are less-than-precise processes. Given the power of pricing, it's easy to become obsessed with finding the "perfect" value-based price. This focus on perfection is amplified by the need to set an exact price—should it be $4.79 or $4.99? My advice is that while prices derived from these two methods are less than perfect, they may be better than the current prices. As an analogy, consider a weight loss program. A highly disciplined daily regiment of consuming less than 2,000 calories per day and running for sixty minutes on a treadmill is a perfect recipe to shed those excess pounds.

That said, focusing on eating right and exercising regularly are positive steps in the right direction and accomplish similar results.

Figure 1-7 ▪ Demand Curve Methodology Pro/Con Matrix

Demand Curve Methodology	Pros	Cons
Market research	• Measures value directly from consumer • Precise • Can be adjusted if competitors' prices change	• Can be expensive • Relatively time-intensive • Less relevant if value changes (because of budget, next-best alternatives, close/extended substitutes, taste/trends, new attributes, complementary products)
Experienced judgment	• Leverages internal expert judgment and actual data points • Easy to adjust analysis if variable affecting value changes • Inexpensive and quick	• Less precise
One-on-one pricing	• Leverages internal expert judgment • Often the only viable option for new products • Easy to adjust analysis if variables affecting value change • Inexpensive and quick	• Less precise

SIX REASONS WHY A VALUE-BASED PRICE MAY CHANGE

Setting a value-based price is an important and necessary start to better pricing. But keep in mind that a product's value changes over time. The key to pricing for profits and growth is to adjust product prices as their value changes. Much like stocks in financial markets, the value of a product fluctuates.

SETTING A VALUE-BASED PRICE: THE ORANGE MYPOD PLAYER

Here's a simple example of how to set a value-based price using the one-on-one pricing methodology. Suppose Orange, a hypothetical technology company, charges $100 for its myPod MP3 player (by using its "that's how we always do it" method of marking up costs by 33%). The myPod's $75 manufacturing cost translates into a $100 price. However, if it establishes a value-based price, the process is as follows:

1. *Identify the myPod's target customers and their next-best alternative, and use that price as a starting point.* In this case, the next-best alternative is the $80 Apple iPod.

2. *Determine how the myPod player differs from the iPod.* Orange offers a sleeker style and hipper brand.

3. *Use experienced judgment from field experience to determine what discount or premium the average customer will pay for an Orange myPod player relative to the $80 iPod.* Assume experienced minds agree a $30 premium is warranted.

4. *Ensure that using the $80 iPod price as a starting point is realistic.* If this price is too high—that is, customers are not willing to pay it—then it is not valid to use. But the $80 price is reasonable, as many iPods are being sold for that amount.

This leads to a $110 value-based price ($80 starting point plus $30 premium). This additional $10 is pure profit, resulting in a 40% increase in profit margin ($10 in new profits added to the $25 of current profits).

These six core forces can change a product's value:

Consumer budget. Reduced income typically results in a lower willingness to pay for premium attributes, as well as cutting nonessential purchases. Conversely, an increase in income results in customers being able to pay more for better quality or premium attributes, and they are also more likely to purchase nonessential luxury goods. Wal-Mart's increase in net profits during the recent recession is in part credited to its stores stocking lower-priced merchandise during a time when consumers' budgets were tightening.[10]

Next-best alternatives. New competitors may enter the market or existing competitors may change their attributes and/or prices. Also note that when setting a price nationally, a product's next-best alternative may differ by region. There are many regional premium players in the ice cream industry. Graeter's, based in my hometown of Cincinnati, garnered talk show host Oprah Winfrey's endorsement as the best ice cream that she'd ever tasted.[11] In the few Midwestern markets that it serves, Graeter's should be considered a viable next-best alternative to premium brands such as Ben & Jerry's.

Close and extended substitutes for consumers. Changes in both close and extended substitutes can affect value. Returning to Ben & Jerry's premium pricing, a price decrease of a close substitute (Dove), as well as a more drastic discount of a supermarket private label (extended substitute), can affect the value customers place on a pint of Ben & Jerry's Cherry Garcia.

Consumer taste/trends. A shift in customer preferences affects the prices they are willing to pay. An advertising campaign to bolster a company's brand often enables prices to be raised. Also, the growing green movement has customers placing increased value on environmentally friendly products.

New attributes. Earning a "best of" award or a favorable critical review increases value. Additional features or formulations that support a marketing claim of "new and improved" can also boost the price that consumers are willing to pay.

Complementary products. If the price of a product used in conjunction with another changes, this affects value. Consider the complementary demand between gasoline and car prices. The American Lease Guide found that after gas crossed the $4 mark in the United States, the resale values of fuel-efficient compact cars increased by as much as 22%, while values of some gas-guzzling SUVs sank by 27%.[12]

Any shift in these six variables changes the value customers place on a product and thus also affects the "right price." This is why it's important to reevaluate a product's value regularly.

STANDING UP FOR AND CAPTURING VALUE AT SMUGMUG

Just because the competition is charging low prices or giving products away for free doesn't mean that you have to do the same for your
product. This is the lesson demonstrated by Chris MacAskill, the cofounder and president of SmugMug, a website that allows its members
to share their photos and buy prints.

The energy that Chris devotes to SmugMug reflects the importance that photos have had in his own life. His family moved constantly
throughout his childhood, and pictures brought back memories of good
times. "My grandfather shot 16 mm films in the 1930s. As a kid, my
family would watch these films and we all would laugh. I never forgot
those times," he reminisced.[13] Given these experiences, he believes that
taking and sharing pictures "has an impact on families."

SmugMug was founded during tough economic and market conditions. In 2002, capital was scarce, and the photo-sharing market was
dominated by well-known brands such as Kodak, Snapfish, and Shut-
terfly. Oh, and one minor detail: SmugMug was going to charge for its
services, while its well-entrenched rivals didn't. "What part of Google
don't you understand?" business associates chided him. After Chris
excitedly laid out his plans to close friends, some smiled, shook their
heads, and sighed, "We'll say a prayer for you." Starting in his family's
five-bedroom Silicon Valley home, where blow dryers and the vacuum
regularly blew circuit breakers, Chris marched forward.[14]

If your product is better than the competition's, you are entitled to
profit from its higher quality. Ask Chris why customers should pay for
his service when rivals are free and he evangelizes about the value of
his site relative to its next-best alternatives: "Our pictures are bigger,
sharper, full screen, have unique backgrounds, and our storage is unlimited. Plus we don't have ads next to your pictures or require your
friends to sign up to view your pictures." SmugMug also hosts a vibrant
community of fellow photography aficionados.

"Pricing is the single most important strategy at SmugMug," Chris told me. "If you make someone look good, they'll pay for it. SmugMug showcases our customers' life stories. How do you put a price on that?" Customers agree with Chris' sentiments. While well-known sites including America Online Pictures, Yahoo! Photos, and Sony Image Station have closed their doors, SmugMug is thriving. SmugMug has a customer base of more than 300,000 members who each pay between $39.95 and $149.95 annually. SmugMug's success illustrates the fundamental principle of pricing: know your product attributes and then stand up for and capture the value of your products and services.

VALUE-BASED PRICING: THE FIRST (AND FUNDAMENTAL) STEP TO REAPING A PRICING WINDFALL

By viewing and setting prices to capture value, you'll be ahead of 90% of the companies that call me seeking pricing advice. Creating a value-based price should be the foundation of every company's pricing strategy.

I've found that companies are quick to accept that their product is "just like the competition's" and set a similar price. However, most products provide a unique value to consumers. Understanding how customers benefit from a product is integral to better pricing. At first blush, the profit potential seemed low for fly ash or a new product entering an industry where competitors were not charging for their services. But as Olivier Biebuyck and Chris MacAskill proved, focusing on how their products differed from their customers' next-best alternatives generated significant new profits and growth.

KEY TAKEAWAYS

CAPTURE VALUE BY THINKING LIKE A CUSTOMER

- Better pricing involves setting prices that capture the value of a product. Street vendors increase the price of umbrellas the moment it looks like rain, which illustrates that pricing is about capturing value, not marking up costs or focusing on margins.
- Two methods to set value-based prices: one-on-one pricing (selling one product to one customer), and multicustomer pricing (selling more than one product to many different customers). The primary difference between these two methods is that multicustomer pricing requires thinking about and creating a demand curve for a product.
- One-on-one pricing involves (1) identifying target customers, (2) identifying the next-best alternative and using its price as a starting point, (3) determining a product's differences relative to its next-best alternative, (4) calculating a product's value based on its differentiation, and (5) doing a reality check on the price of the next-best alternative.
- Characteristics that differentiate products include brand, quality, attributes, service, ease of purchase, and style.
- Different customers have different subjective and objective valuations for a product. Because of these unique valuations, some customers are willing to pay more than others.
- The four steps of multicustomer pricing are: (1) identify the target consumer's next-best alternative, reality-check its price, and use that price as a starting point, (2) determine product differences, (3) create a demand curve based on the concept that different customers have different valuations for a product's

uniqueness, and (4) undertake a profit maximizer analysis to find the most profitable value-based price.

- Profit maximizer analysis: calculate revenues, costs, and profits at price levels spanning high to low, and then select the price associated with the highest profits.
- A demand curve can be generated through (1) market research, (2) experienced judgment, or (3) one-on-one pricing.
- Note that a value-based price changes if any of the following variables change: (1) consumer budget, (2) next-best alternatives for consumers, (3) close and extended substitutes for consumers, (4) consumer taste/trends, (5) new attributes, and (6) complementary products. Any shift in these variables changes the value that customers place on a product, and hence affects the value-based price.

PART TWO

The Strategy of Pricing

A VALUE-BASED PRICE IS JUST THE BEGINNING

Setting a value-based price is just the first step in creating a comprehensive pricing strategy for a product. It is the base of a company's pricing strategy and the price that most customers will end up paying. That said, there are several additional opportunities to use price to profit and grow.

In virtually every facet of business, companies develop strategies based on the truism that their customers differ from each other. Diverse customers are courted with a variety of products (different styles, colors, add-ons), a mix of marketing strategies, and multiple distribution points. However, when it comes to pricing, most companies behave as though their customers are identical by setting just one price for each product.

The epiphany to better pricing is to understand—actually, to embrace—the same insight that companies use to create strategies and profit in other areas of their business: a wide variety of customers are interested in buying their product, and these customers differ from each other. These differences are what make pricing a creative business strategy instead of a search for one "perfect" price.

PRICING STRATEGIES THAT EARN
HIGHER MARGINS AND SELL TO MORE CUSTOMERS

The strategy of pricing involves acknowledging that customers have different pricing needs and then making efforts to profit from these differences. Customers differ in three primary ways:

1. *Desire a different pricing plan.* Some customers don't like a particular pricing plan (instead of owning outright, they prefer to lease, for instance). Chapter 2 presents the strategy of pick-a-plan, which involves offering new pricing plans to serve new customers, and offers sixteen pick-a-plan tactics.
2. *Have unique needs or value a product differently.* Chapter 3 is dedicated to the strategy of versioning, which involves offering a series of slightly different products based on one core product. These versions are profitable for two reasons. First, products can meet unique customer needs. Poland Spring water sells a series of different product sizes to meet its customers' unique needs. Its delivery service of 5-gallon water bottles (which sit on top of freestanding water cooler bases) serves businesses and families. It also sells 2.5-gallon jugs at grocery stores; these are meant to be kept in home refrigerators for daily use. And its 16-ounce bottles, often sold at convenience stores, can quench thirst on the run. Second, versions serve and profit from customers with different valuations. Offering good, better, and best products (accompanied by good, better, and best profit margins) allows customers to choose the version that best fits their valuation and allows a company to profit accordingly. Chapter 3 explains seventeen versioning tactics.
3. *Value a product differently.* As discussed in Chapter 1, customers value products differently. Differential pricing, discussed in Chapter 4, is the strategy of charging different prices to different customers for the same product. This chapter offers seventeen differential pricing tactics.

Figure Part 2-1

CUSTOMER DIFFERENCE AND ASSOCIATED STRATEGIES

CUSTOMER DIFFERENCE		STRATEGY
Desire a different pricing plan	➡	Pick-a-Plan
Have unique product needs	➡	Versioning
Value a product differently	➡	Differential Pricing

For clarity, let me define how I use the terms *strategy* and *tactic*. A strategy is a category of initiatives designed to achieve an overall goal. Tactics are individual initiatives used to achieve the goal of a strategy. The strategy of pick-a-plan covers the overall concept of offering new pricing plans to attract new customers. Pick-a-plan tactics are initiatives such as renting and interval ownership.

Figure Part 2-2

STRATEGY VERSUS TACTIC

STRATEGY: category of initiatives designed to achieve an overall goal.

TACTIC: individual initiatives used to achieve the goal of a strategy.

THE PRICING BLOSSOM STRATEGY

To capitalize on these three fundamental customer differences, companies need to create a comprehensive *pricing blossom strategy*, which features multiple prices. The foundation of a pricing blossom is built on setting a value-based price and then adding pick-a-plan, versioning, and differential pricing strategies.

Figure Part 2-3
PRICING BLOSSOM STRATEGY

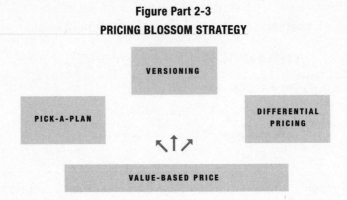

Not every company is in a position to offer all three strategies. Some can offer more than others. In general:

Every company can set a value-based price.
Most companies can employ versioning and differential pricing strategies.
Some companies can implement pick-a-plan strategies.

PRICING BLOSSOM PREVIEW

To preview what is on the way in the next four chapters, as well as how to start thinking about a comprehensive pricing strategy, here are examples of a pricing blossom for a service (long-distance phone service) and a product (automobile).

LONG-DISTANCE PHONE SERVICE

- *Value-based price.* Start off with value-based long-distance prices for customers without a discount plan.

- *Pick-a-plan.* Offer unlimited home long-distance service and prepaid phone service cards (sold at convenience stores).

- *Versioning.* Provide customers the option of using a credit card, having an 800 number, or buying a lower-quality (and discount-priced) VoIP (voice over Internet protocol) service.

- *Differential pricing.* Sell discount options such as Verizon's Five Cents Plan. For a $6 monthly fee, calls in the United States are 5 cents a minute.

Figure Part 2-4
LONG DISTANCE SERVICE

PICK-A-PLAN	VERSIONING	DIFFERENTIAL PRICING
• Unlimited	• Credit card	• Several plans
• Prepaid	• 800 #	
	• VoIP	

VALUE-BASED PRICE
• Value-based price

AUTOMOBILES

- *Value-based price.* Create a value-based price for the base car model.

- *Pick-a-plan.* Offer leases and financing deals.

- *Versioning.* Roll out premium and sporty versions of the base car, as well as the options for rust warranty and antilock brakes.

- *Differential prices.* Lower prices for seniors and students. Run promotions such as $1,000 off over the Fourth of July. Negotiate unique prices for each customer.

Figure Part 2-5
VEHICLES

PICK-A-PLAN	VERSIONING	DIFFERENTIAL PRICING
• Lease	• Sporty	• Student
• Financing deals	• Premium	• Promotions
	• Warranty	• Negotiation

VALUE-BASED PRICE
• Value-based price

2

Pick-a-Plan

---

rowing a business can be as straightforward as offering a new
pricing plan that attracts new customers. Let me bring things
down to ground level. In fact, let's start *below* the ground. Because of
their proven ability to generate growth, rolling out new pricing plans is
a top priority at Terminix, the pest control company.

Did you know that termites cause more than $5 billion of property
damage in the United States annually?[1] Or that a mature colony of
termites (which eat twenty-four hours a day, seven days a week) can
devour up to a pound of wood in one day?[2] Protection from infestation
is a service that all homeowners should consider.

Historically, termite control services and their pricing have been
fairly standard. A homeowner discovers termites, then calls a pest control specialist. After a treatment, homeowners have the option to pay an
annual fee that covers regular inspections and retreatment if necessary.
Roughly 3 million of 75 million U.S. households purchase some type of
ongoing termite protection.

This business model has served the industry well for decades.

However, the industry is reaching maturity, with limited growth opportunities and declining industry sales. Confronting this reality and its potential long-term repercussions, Terminix COO Tom Brackett told his executive team, "We need to be disruptive; we need to do it right; and we need to do it now." So what did Steve Good, senior vice president of business development at Terminix, and his colleagues focus on to combat the ills of a declining industry? A new pricing strategy.

"Instead of slugging it out with competitors for jobs at residences infested by termites, we focused our efforts on the 72 million homes in the United States [without termites] that could benefit by purchasing protection," Steve explained.[3] There's good reason for these 72 million homeowners to be concerned about termites. On average, termites cause $3,000 in damage (which most home insurance policies don't cover), and it typically costs between $900 and $1,800 to rid a house of them. Through focus group interviews, Steve found that termites were "out of sight and out of mind" for most homeowners. "Why replace your water heater before it breaks?" he pointed out. Homeowners were interested in "one price, with no additional costs," and valued the idea of being "protected" from termites.

Steve left the focus groups with the idea that Terminix had to "provide consumers with a choice." This insight, along with the company's eighty years of historical data on termite damage incident rates, led his team to create a termite inspection and protection plan. Homeowners would pay an annual fee that covers a comprehensive inspection, treatments (if necessary), and a guarantee from Terminix to pay for any damage caused by termites. This new service differs from standard industry protection plans in two important ways. First, homeowners do not have to pay for an expensive termite treatment to qualify for this protection. And unlike most plans, it covers all costs to repair any termite damage. Consumers have embraced and are benefiting from this new pricing plan.

Terminix is also benefiting from this new pricing plan. In an industry characterized by declining sales, within just a year of launch Terminix was able to increase the sale of renewable termite plans by

12%, in great part because of this new inspection and protection plan. Additionally, the company's sales force loves the plan. If an inspection by a concerned homeowner yields no evidence of termites, they still have a product to offer. And finally, the plan offers new distribution channel opportunities via strategic alliances. Terminix is partnering with financial and real estate companies to offer the inspection and protection plan to their clients. With all of these successes, Steve and his colleagues are looking to offer creative protection solutions for the other twenty-six types of insects, that Terminix provides treatment for.

What I find so compelling about Terminix's strategy is its focus and success in activating many of its 72 million potential customers. A new pricing plan opened up a fresh segment of customers and renewed sales in a declining market. This chapter presents pricing plans specifically focused on activating "dormant customers," just as Steve and his colleagues are doing.

PICK-A-PLAN

Of all the pricing strategies in this book, pick-a-plan is my favorite. I like to hit business home runs, and that is exactly what pick-a-plan can do. This pricing strategy leverages committed investments to bring a product to market and create interest from customers. One barrier to purchase has been that potential customers may not like the current pricing plan. Instead of buying, some may prefer to lease. These dormant customers (who are already intrigued with a product) can be drawn in with a new pricing option. Pick-a-plan, like all of the pricing concepts and tactics I discuss in this book, is applicable to a wide spectrum of products and customers of varying income levels.

Offering a new pricing strategy can open the door for new customers to purchase and generate blockbuster growth. A new pick-a-plan pricing tactic can be so powerful and effective that many times companies base their entire business on it.

Figure 2-1

PICK-A-PLAN PRICING TACTICS

OWNERSHIP ALTERNATIVES	UNCERTAIN VALUE	PRICE ASSURANCE	FINANCIAL & OTHER CONSTRAINTS
• Interval ownership	• Success fees	• Flat rate	• Financing
• Lease	• Licenses	• Peace of mind guarantee	• Job loss protection
• Rental	• Auctions	• All-you-can-eat	• Layaway
• Netflix model	• Future to buy options	• Two part: high/low pricing	• Prepaid

In this chapter, I discuss sixteen pick-a-plan tactics, which can be categorized into themes: offering new ownership alternatives, alleviating concerns over uncertain product value, providing price assurance, and overcoming financial and other constraints. Any one or combination of these pick-a-plan tactics has the power to produce a pricing windfall.

OWNERSHIP ALTERNATIVES

Some customers are interested in a particular product but can't afford or don't need to own it. A new type of ownership program can be the right stimulus to move these customers from store aisles to the checkout counter. Pick-a-plan ownership pricing tactics include interval ownership, leasing, renting, and the Netflix model.

Interval Ownership

"I don't need to own the whole product, but I am interested in owning part of it."

Interval ownership is the concept of parsing a whole product into smaller ownership units and selling these incremental units individually. Chances are that you've received mailings promoting a 3-night, 4-day vacation for $199 or experienced in-person solicitations in resort areas offering dinner for two in return for taking a ninety-minute tour. These time-share promotions market the application of interval ownership pricing to properties. Condominiums are divvied up into fifty-two weeks and each week is sold individually. Buyers pay an up-front purchase price and are assessed an annual fee to cover maintenance expenses. Many vacationers find it preferable to purchase a week or two of a condominium rather than fully owning a property that might only be used sparingly. An outright purchase also carries the burdens of a higher financial commitment (in both up-front costs as well as annual maintenance fees) and chores associated with keeping a condo in good shape. Interval condominium ownership is a pricing plan that has caught on with vacationers as the number of newly constructed time-share units grew by approximately 15% a year.[4] Ernst & Young estimated there are 4.1 million time-share owners in the United States.[5]

While high-pressure sales and dire warnings to "sign now because this deal may not be available tomorrow" occasionally crop up in association with time-share sales, the industry has gained respectability. Today, well-known lodging companies such as Hilton and Ritz-Carlton offer a range of purchasing options designed to appeal to a wide spectrum of customers. A two-bedroom condominium at the Hilton Grand Vacations Club in Orlando, Florida, sold for $20,990 a week plus $985 in annual fees.[6] At the higher end of the spectrum, three weeks of ownership at Ritz-Carlton Club properties can run as high as $840,000.[7] The evolution of the time-share pricing tactic from selling a week of a condominium in resort areas with few amenities to high-end residences in the Caribbean that provide premium services (even going so far as to set out an owner's personal pictures prior to arrival) demonstrates the applicability of this pricing tactic to a range of income levels.

Leasing

"I don't want to own your product, but I am interested in contracting to use it for an extended time period."

Leasing involves purchasing the right to use a product such as a vehicle or heavy machinery for a fixed period. Payments are generally made monthly. Then, at the end of the lease, the product is either returned to the lessor or purchased at a previously agreed-upon price. The mechanics behind leasing for a company include forecasting the product's value at the end of the lease and setting payments to cover this depreciation cost. Lease payments have little to do with a product's selling price. Instead, they are based on how much a product depreciates over the lease term. According to *Consumer Reports*, the average vehicle depreciation over three years is 45%.[8] However, some cars (such as a Lexus RX) hold their value better than others (a Mercury Grand Marquis, for example).[9] For a given selling price, the higher the depreciation rate, the greater the lease payment.

There are several customer benefits to leasing. For the same car, monthly lease payments are usually lower than loan payments (the rule of thumb is 30–60% less). Thus, an equivalent monthly lease payment allows customers to drive a more expensive vehicle, which they often choose to do. Dealers prefer leases because they make more money from expensive cars. Leases are also well suited to customers who enjoy driving newer vehicles: every two or three years, when the lease is up, just drop the car off at the dealer's lot and pick up a new one. And finally, one benefit of driving a relatively new leased car is that it is covered by a manufacturer's warranty, which eliminates most maintenance bills. Not surprisingly, leasing is a popular strategy and in 2007 accounted for 20% of Ford and Chrysler's unit sales.[10]

Leasing is particularly popular for luxury cars. In August 2009, 32% of import luxury vehicle brand (Acura, Audi, BMW, Lexus, and Mercedes) customers in the United States opted to lease. In addition, a

Texas Cadillac dealership claims that leasing used to account for 65% of its business.[11]

The wrinkle to leasing for companies, of course, is forecasting a product's residual value. There is uncertainty in estimating the value of a vehicle in a few years. In the second quarter of 2008, due to a declining economy and higher gas prices, Ford reported that the residual value of its twenty-four- and thirty-six-month leases were down, on average, by $2,400 and $2,700, respectively, compared to the previous year.[12] In part because of these lower residual values, Ford announced that its financing division had to write down a $2.1 billion loss.[13]

Rental

"I'd like to use your product for a short period of time."

The rental option allows customers to use a product for a period shorter than leases typically offer. Beverly Hills Rent-a-Car equips its clients to fit into the Hollywood scene of sunny days, palm trees, and flashy cars. Its customer base, which includes tourists, royal families, corporate executives, and movie stars, comes for the company's exotic fleet, which includes Lamborghinis, Ferraris, and its marquee $7,500-a-day Rolls-Royce convertible. These customers don't want to purchase or lease a car. They just want to revel in a few days of glitz.

An emerging growth area in the car rental business (which typically hires out cars for one to seven days) involves even shorter rentals. Zipcar pioneered the short-term rental market by offering rentals for as little as sixty minutes. This new pricing tactic activates new customers such as urban residents and university students who want to run local errands. Drawn by Zipcar's success, major rental companies such as Enterprise, Hertz, and U-Haul are entering this hourly vehicle rental market.[14]

One of the biggest challenges for the textbook publishing industry is the resale market. At the end of the semester, many students resell their books on the used-book market. Thus, these students in essence rent a book, with the fee being the difference between their purchase price and the resale price. The downside for publishers is that they are cut out of the profits from selling another copy to a future student next semester.

The thriving resale textbook market demonstrates that *some* students prefer to rent their books. In one of the most popular blogs on my website (www.pricingforprofit.com), I advocate that instead of ignoring this market, publishers need to embrace their customers' pricing preferences. There's profit to be made by serving both the rental and purchase markets. For, say, 50% of the list price, students could rent a book from the publisher for the semester. At the end of the semester, students return it to the publisher on campus or via mail.

This proposition is win-win for both students and book publishers. Students will benefit from a formalized rental service and know the fee up front (instead of perhaps learning at the end of the semester that the resale price is low due to weak demand or a new forthcoming edition). Publishers win by continuing to profit from the value of their textbooks. Additionally, publishers can offer options such as renting a new hardcover, a used hardcover, or a one-time-use paperback (which would be destroyed when returned) at different rental prices. This pricing strategy can help stem the resale "bleeding" that has long plagued the textbook publishing industry. Renting opens a product to new customers who want to use it for a short time and also curbs profit-draining resale markets. Those who prefer to own their textbooks can continue to make outright purchases.

Unfortunately for publishers, independent companies are starting to offer textbook rentals. Chegg, a start-up company, rents textbooks for a fraction of their purchase price. As is common when a new pricing plan resonates with customers, Chegg has enjoyed strong growth. With over $10 million in revenues in all of 2008, the company surpassed that mark in January 2009 alone.[15] With such strong consumer interest, top-tier Silicon Valley venture capitalists are investing in Chegg's belief that renting will become an important pricing plan in the textbook industry.

The Netflix Model

"I'm interested in renting your products, and I value variety."

The Netflix model is a type of rental that involves paying a fixed monthly price for a set number of products with exchange privileges. Consider Netflix's three-movie plan. For a flat monthly fee, a subscriber can rent three movies at a time. Movies can be exchanged by mail in a prepaid envelope. Upon receipt, the next movie in their film queue is sent. Movies can be kept for as long (or short) as the subscriber wishes, and there's no limit to the number of movie exchanges. As a result, it's possible to receive a new movie in the mail nearly every day from Netflix.

This business model has changed the DVD rental market. Movie watchers appreciate that their DVDs arrive and are returned by mail (which eliminates driving to and from their video stores). But just as important, subscribers value the idea that one price covers unlimited rentals and eliminates late fees. Today, 15 million people in the United States subscribe to services that offer this type of movie rental.[16] This pricing tactic is attractive to customer segments that value variety and renting instead of owning products. Tapping audiences with similar needs, companies are using the Netflix model for products such as handbags, books, video games, and expensive cars.

UNCERTAIN VALUE

Sometimes it's difficult for consumers to estimate the ultimate value of a product. In rapidly changing technological environments, it is fair to question whether a great product today will be obsolete tomorrow. Similarly, a seller may make grand pledges, but it's uncertain whether the product will deliver the promised value. Pricing tactics that reduce the value uncertainty of a product include success fees, licensing, auctions, and future purchase options.

Success Fees

"I'm interested in your product but am concerned about its performance."

Success fees are often used in pricing scenarios that involve uncertainty or are highly dependent on the future efforts of one party. This strategy involves a base price plus a bonus if a key success metric is achieved. The party selling the product with uncertain value is given incentives to perform to the best of its ability. Setting prices in this manner shares the risk of uncertain outcomes. It's a gamble for a baseball team to sign a contract with a forty-one-year-old player because of declining physical skills and the increased chance of injury associated with age. Curt Schilling, considered one of the best postseason pitchers in the history of baseball, faced this situation. To hedge their risk, the Boston Red Sox signed Schilling to a one-year deal that offered a base salary of $8 million with a potential extra $6 million in success fee opportunities. One such success fee covers staying in shape. Schilling will receive $2 million if he maintains his weight (based on six random weigh-ins). "The responsibility falls on me," Schilling pointed out about his weight success fee. "There are 2 million reasons for me to reach my weight goal."[17] Theo Epstein, a Red Sox executive, revealed how success fees helped handle Schilling's uncertain value: "If there's a downside or things don't work out next year then $8 million seems reasonable under that scenario. If everything goes right, if he gets himself in great shape and pitches the whole season, then we're comfortable with the higher number (up to $14 million), which is why the contract is structured that way."[18]

Law firms are also incorporating success fees into their pricing strategy to attract new customers. Responding to concerns brought up by midsize entrepreneurial companies, the law firm Holland and Knight retooled its pricing strategy. For some cases, the law firm charges discounted hourly fees in return for a success fee if the outcome is in their client's favor.[19] This pricing structure ensures that lawyers working on a case are energized and incentivized to win the case.

Licensing

"I love your product, but I'm unsure about its long-term commercial value."

Licensing is the strategy of allowing third parties to use intellectual property (trademarks, patents, or technology) in return for financial compensation tied to its value. Many times it's challenging to estimate a product's value to end users. The value of owning an Ace Hardware franchise located at a high-traffic intersection is probably greater than that of one in a remote suburban strip mall. How should Ace Hardware charge its franchises to capture these types of differing valuations? Similarly, it's unknown to publishers whether J. K. Rowling's next novel will be as big as the last book in her Harry Potter series. You can imagine all of the effort that would be needed to negotiate a fair price in these uncertain business transactions, and the distinct probability of not reaching a deal. To avoid this situation, one option is to license the rights to use intellectual property in return for a percentage of the revenues that it helps generate. This licensing plan captures the value of the intellectual property, reduces the risk for third-party buyers, and allows sellers to participate in the potential upside.

Silicon Valley electronics company Tessera Technologies developed an innovative licensing strategy for its chip packaging technology. This technology improves silicon chips by making them smaller and more reliable. One challenge that Tessera and its licensees faced was that standard licensing techniques such as a royalty per chip or a cut of revenues might inadequately capture the value of Tessera's intellectual property. Chips continuously become more powerful, for instance. A single chip tomorrow could replace four or five today. Thus, charging a per-chip royalty might undervalue the contribution of Tessera's technology to the licensee's products and lead to lower license revenues for Tessera as the reliability improvements from Tessera's technology became more pronounced and important. Additionally, chip prices can fluctuate so widely that charging royalties based on a percentage of revenues could cause significant discrepancies between licensees and result in lower royalties for Tessera.

Tessera's negotiations led to an innovative focus on the correlation between the potency of a chip and the number of electrical connections to the chip within the package. Generally, the more powerful the chip, the more electrical connections it will have. Royalties paid by Tessera's licensees often focus on the number of electrical connections within the chip, rather than on units, average selling price, or other more common metrics. Charging a royalty per electrical connection not only better captured the value of Tessera's technology based on the enhancement to the chips but also shielded the company and its licensees from dramatic changes in royalties due to fluctuations in chip prices.

Auctions

"I'm interested in purchasing, but your product's value is too uncertain."

Auctions involve accepting bids for a product and selling to the highest bidder at the end of a fixed period. You are probably familiar with an auction through buying or selling a product on eBay or participating in a fast-paced live auction. Why do sellers prefer auctions? Sales are quick and they establish prices for hard-to-value products such as the previously discussed lunch with Warren Buffett. In addition, knowing what others are willing to pay for a product with subjective value provides some reassurance to bidders that they aren't overpaying.

Take housing as an example. Since it's so challenging to establish what the right price is in today's housing market, auctions are becoming an increasingly popular selling tool. As of fall 2008, only 53% of the 20,000 condominiums built in Miami since 2003 had been sold.[20] In these market conditions, it's almost futile to keep lowering prices in hopes of finding the right price that will trigger a sale. Consumers are waiting for a lower price, as no one wants to overpay. In tough real estate markets such as Miami, developers are now auctioning off blocks of condominiums rather than individually selling them as they had before. An auction establishes a current market price and seals deals. This outcome is better than a continuing loss. In general, winning bids at housing auctions are roughly two-thirds of preconstruction sale prices.[21] Highlighting the benefits of using an auction, one Florida real estate agent explained, "Why try to catch a falling knife? Let it hit the ground. That's what an auction does."[22]

Auctions aren't limited to establishing prices for downtrodden products. They also establish value in more vibrant markets. Consider the auction of *The Kingdom*, a piece of art by popular British artist Damien Hirst. This piece, an almost eight-foot tiger shark situated in a black-framed glass tank of formaldehyde, was sold after its bidding peaked at $17 million in September 2008.[23] Reinforcing the concept that price has little to do with cost, Mr. Hirst had reportedly paid an Australian shark hunter only $200 for the shark carcass.[24] An auction establishes the value of a piece today, provides insight on its future resale price, and can contribute to the overall value of an artist's brand. Since the price of artwork is highly subjective, fervent bidding also stokes the bragging rights: "Oh, it's part of my collection."

Future Purchase Options

"I'm not sure if I'll use your product in the future. However, I am willing to pay a fee today to lock in a price for tomorrow if I need it."

Future purchase options offer consumers the right, but not the obligation, to purchase a product in the future. Sometimes consumers don't know if they'll need a product in the future. However, they value a guarantee of being able to buy the product if they end up wanting it.

American Community is using a unique health insurance option pricing plan to target the 40% of uninsured Americans who are nineteen to thirty-four years old and healthy, the fastest-growing segment of the uninsured population. Feeling healthy and invincible, many of these potential customers shun health insurance because their risk/reward analysis deems the price too high. For a monthly premium as low as $88, American Community offers insurance with deductibles ranging from zero to $500 and annual benefit caps of $1,000 to $5,000. Should a policyholder become ill, he or she has the option to activate a policy with a $5 million benefit for $9,000 to $10,000 a year.[25] The pricing features of this insurance are the focal points of its marketing campaign, which uses taglines such as "Coverage on Demand" and "Pay as You Go." With a low premium and the option to buy full coverage in the event of an illness, this insurance policy lets the uninsured hedge their health costs. This new pricing plan activates (and covers) customers who had decided that most current insurance plans don't work for them.

PRICE CERTAINTY

Few customers enjoy uncertainty, especially when it comes to price and its impact on their budgets. Reducing or eliminating price uncertainty appeals to customers and provides a competitive edge for companies. Pricing strategies that provide certainty include flat rates, peace-of-mind guarantee, all-you-can-eat, and two-part high/low pricing.

Flat Rate

"I don't appreciate the anxiety of watching the hours for my project rack up; I prefer a set price."

Flat-rate pricing offers to undertake a project for a fixed fee. Few of us enjoy the watching-the-clock neurosis that often accompanies a time-based pricing agreement. These contracts offer carte blanche to bill, and there's little incentive for the provider to economize. The customer wonders, "Are they padding the bill? Is it worth it to me to call with a question? Are they taking the quickest route? Are they loafing?" In these situations, most consumers appreciate and value the security of a fixed price that eliminates the concerns of uncontrollable costs.

Law firms are starting to profit by addressing this anxiety. The Ambrose Law Group, a Portland boutique law firm, has switched from billing by the hour to fixed fees for many of its projects. This switch in its pricing was a key reason why the law firm increased its profits by 90% a year after making the change.[26] Since buyers prefer certainty, offering a flat rate provides an advantage when competing for business. Another law firm, Jackson Lewis, was awarded all of Pfizer's employment-related litigation work in great part due to its willingness to agree to a fixed fee. Commenting on the decision to work with Jackson Lewis, a Pfizer executive noted: "Jackson Lewis got it because they recognized that we needed to find some alternative to billing by the hour."[27]

Peace-of-Mind Guarantee

"For psychological and planning purposes, I value locking in product prices for the future."

A peace-of-mind guarantee is the option of protecting consumers from price fluctuations by offering a fixed price for a given time period. When home heating oil prices swing wildly, one Massachusetts oil supplier observed, "People are scared and they should be."[28] A popular pricing strategy that has struck a chord with consumers is a home heating oil protection plan. Plans such as these guarantee a fixed price for a certain quantity of oil throughout the heating season. Once a customer strikes an agreement with a local oil company, the company purchases the estimated amount of oil that customer will use from its suppliers. This strategy provides consumers peace of mind in the face of market price fluctuations and allows them to plan for this expense. This guaranteed price strategy is also popular for key business inputs. Due to the uncertainty of beef prices, Morton's, the high-end steak-house chain, locked in purchase contracts for 70% of its prime beef and roughly half of its fillet needs to protect it from price volatility that might affect its signature products.[29]

A twist on fixed prices is capped prices. While fixed prices bring certainty, some customers worry that prices will go lower, and they want to benefit from these declines. To satisfy these customers, many home oil companies offer price cap programs. Once a customer signs up, a local oil company purchases oil from its suppliers, as well as a hedge contract. This hedge pays off, for instance, if prices decrease 5 cents or more from the current contracted price. As a result, customers not only receive a guarantee of maximum price but also benefit if prices decrease during the contracted period.[30]

While both peace-of-mind and flat-rate plans benefit companies (who get new customers attracted by the pricing plan) and their customers (who are assured of some certainty), the plans are different. Flat-rate pricing provides assurance in situations where costs are uncertain, such as the number of hours necessary to complete a project. Peace-of-mind pricing provides a guarantee against fluctuations in a product price.

All-You-Can-Eat

"I'd like to use and/or sample as much as I want without having to consider every purchase."

All-you-can-eat is a pricing plan that involves paying one price for the freedom to enjoy all that you can eat or use. This pricing plan targets customers who value (1) not having to think about every extra purchase, (2) the variety of picking and choosing (water skiing, scuba, and volleyball at all-inclusive resorts, or everything from eggs to sushi at brunch buffets), and (3) the certainty of a fixed price. Similar to the other pricing plans in this chapter, this strategy can be applied to a variety of products ranging from dinner buffets and Internet service to upscale all-inclusive vacation resorts. Customers of varying incomes appreciate the virtues of this pricing tactic. Families on a budget enjoy the all-you-can-eat aspect of the $6.99 breakfast buffet at Old Country Buffet restaurants as do the upscale gourmands who consume as much caviar as they please at the $68 Sunday brunch at the Four Seasons Philadelphia.

Of course, a key drawback of an all-you-can-eat pricing plan for companies is the customer who overconsumes. Bandwidth-clogging customers who watch streaming videos or play Web-based games can overwhelm Internet providers. Cable Internet provider Time Warner estimates that 5% of its customers account for more than 50% of its network use.[31] All-you-can-eat pricing plans are profitable only if these profit drainers are balanced by low-volume customers who pay a premium for not having to think about every transaction as they consume.

Firms that use this strategy also need to ensure the proper supply logistics. The restaurant chain Applebee's learned this lesson the hard way. Riblets (tips of small bones from a hog's back) are a signature item at Applebee's. While the popular chain strives to offer an annual all-you-can-eat riblet promotion, it wasn't able to do so in 2003 due to low supply. Determined to continue this once-a-year tradition, Applebee's bolstered its supply and ran another all-you-can-eat riblets promotion in 2004. This time, however, demand was less than expected. The chain ended up with far too many riblets. Because this excess inventory passed its use-by dates, Applebee's had to take a $2.3 million write-off.[32] Despite these potential downsides, all-you-can-eat is an important pricing plan for companies to consider. Many customers appreciate the freedom to consume or use as much as they want and are willing to pay a premium for this privilege.

Two-Part High/Low Pricing

"To receive everyday low prices, I am willing to pay an up-front fee."

Two-part high/low pricing involves charging an up-front price and then setting low second-part variable prices. The warehouse chain Costco uses this pricing strategy by charging an up-front membership fee (from which it makes profit) and providing discount prices for the products that it retails. Costco sells a unique collection of products ranging from toilet paper (its number-one-selling item, with $375 million in sales annually) and rotisserie chicken (37 million chickens a year) to $80,000 diamond rings.[33] And its shoppers are just as eclectic, ranging from suburban families to elite Washington, D.C., power brokers. Superstar Washington lawyer Robert Bennett throws an annual "Costco party" open house featuring "pigs in blankets, salamis, salmon, shrimp, pâté, and cheese."[34]

Costco's second-part variable prices (food, merchandise) deserve special attention. The retailer pledges that its product prices are no more than 14% above its wholesale costs. This maximum 14% markup is much lower than the normal 25–50% markup at grocery stores and department stores.[35] What's striking is that the company's operating profits are made up primarily of the revenues it brings in from membership sales.[36] In essence, customers pay Costco a membership fee in return for the opportunity to purchase products at its costs (wholesale plus retailing costs). While Costco doesn't offer the lowest price on *all* products, its 14% markup pledge provides its members confidence that they get the best price for *most* products. And for this assurance, 87% of Costco members renew their annual membership.[37]

Entering the competitive printer market, Kodak differentiated its printers with a unique pricing strategy. Bucking the industry convention of setting discount prices for printers and then earning profits from premium-priced replacement ink cartridges, Kodak did the exact opposite by employing two-part high/low pricing. Targeting large-volume customers as well as those upset by high replacement ink prices, Kodak charges 30% more for its printers. However, its ink replacement cartridges are 50% lower in price compared to its rivals.[38] In part because of this distinctive pricing model, Kodak aims to capture as much as 10% of the printer market.[39]

FINANCING AND OTHER CONSTRAINTS

In many cases, customers want to purchase a product but refrain from doing so because of issues associated with finances or the requirements of existing pricing plans. They are able to pay and are fine with the price, but just need help overcoming their obstacles. Pricing tactics related to overcoming these types of constraints include offering financing, job loss protection, layaway, and prepaid options.

Financing

"I love your product but need help structuring payments to meet my budget."

Financing is the option of allowing customers to spread out their payments over time with an annual financing rate that can be as low as 0% (such as "no interest for two years" offers). If a company sells big-ticket items, being sensitive to its customers' monthly cash flow by offering financing plans can generate growth.

The availability of financing can influence purchasing decisions. A close friend was choosing between two well-respected dentists to perform expensive dental work. The tipping point was that one offered financing and the other didn't. Similarly, when a colleague's teenage son started to drive, his auto insurance bill multiplied. Facing a large annual bill, he changed insurance companies primarily because his new insurer offers a structured payment plan that debits his bank account monthly.

Offering two-year no-interest financing for purchases over $999 has been a successful pricing plan for Best Buy. This financing tool is credited with helping the electronics retailer gain higher sales volume and market share over rivals, including Radio Shack and Amazon.[40] Best Buy executive vice president Mike Vitelli observed that some customers were "adding items to their shopping cart so they could hit the $999 minimum purchase."[41]

Financing benefits a wide spectrum of customers and products. Retailer financing plans range from mattress stores promising "no money down and no credit checks" to upscale Pottery Barn stores, which attracted 319,000 cardholders and $164 million in charges in the first six months of the retailer's credit card launch.[42] Other products and services that offer financing run the gamut from furniture stores (where 50 to 60% of customers use in-house financing) to medical care (a McKinsey & Company survey found that roughly 20% of retail health consumers were interested in financing or credit card options).[43]

Why not just put these charges on credit cards such as American Express, Visa, or MasterCard? It is usually easier and cheaper to obtain credit from private-label cards. These financing options are less stringent in their credit history review, more liberal in their credit line, and offer lower interest rates. Some consumers also prefer to segment their purchases. Many use brand-name credit cards for everyday purchases and private-label financing for one-time larger purchases such as an expensive appliance.

Offering the best product or service at a low price may not be enough to sway some consumers. Many purchasing decisions come down to choosing a company that provides the financing that works best with a customer's budget.

Job Loss Protection

"I'm interested in your product but am hesitant to purchase because I am concerned that I may be laid off in the future."

Job loss protection involves sellers canceling a purchase or making monthly payments in the event that a buyer gets laid off. As unemployment increased in 2009, consumers held off making large purchases because they feared losing their jobs. In response, many companies offered pricing plans to stimulate sales by helping to allay these concerns. AutoNation, the chain of new- and used-car dealerships, offered to make up to six months of car payments if a buyer suffers a job loss. Mike Maroone, AutoNation's president and chief operating officer, expected this program to boost sales by 10–15%.[44]

Layaway

"With credit being tight, I am looking for an alternative to financing my purchases."

Layaway is the practice of a retailer putting aside desired items and having customers pay over time. Only after the full price is paid can the product leave the store. If a customer defaults, he or she generally receives a refund less a service fee. For the 2008 holiday season, demand for this pricing plan became so high that Kmart decided to feature its layaway policy in a national advertising plan. Discussing this pricing practice, Kmart's chief marketing officer, Mark Snyder, commented, "While not sexy, layaway became the big idea for Kmart these holidays."[45] The company used the layaway pricing plan as a key differentiator over its two top competitors, Wal-Mart and Target.[46]

Prepaid Plans

"My credit is poor and I'm not eligible for a monthly billing plan." or *"Pricing plans require me to have services I don't need or that don't fit my usage patterns."*

Prepaid plans have customers pay in advance for a product and then let them draw down this credit with usage. Prepaid plans serve the credit-challenged, those who value the discipline of a fixed amount of usage, and consumers who don't want to be tied to a monthly plan with minimums and restrictions. Offering prepaid cards also allows products to be marketed and distributed in more locations (prepaid gift cards for merchandise at clothing retailer Gap are sold at CVS, for example).

Prepaid telephone card usage is much higher than I had thought. Consider a typical August 2002 Sunday in the New York area: 414,000 calls were made to Mexico, 310,000 to the Dominican Republic, and 389,000 calls to Guatemala, Colombia, and El Salvador combined. That's a lot of calls, and these calls were all made by owners of prepaid calling cards sold by the IDT Corporation. *And* these were only the top five destinations of those calling with IDT cards (which sells 15 million such cards per month). *And* IDT is just one of hundreds of prepaid calling card providers, including AT&T and Verizon.[47]

The traditional pricing plan of having a home phone and a monthly long-distance plan doesn't work for everybody. There is a segment of customers who want long-distance service but the current pricing plans don't work for them. These include people who don't have local telephone service (they may not need it or may not have the credit to get it) and the thrifty who don't mind dialing several extra digits. With cards available at retailers ranging from Wal-Mart to local bodegas, this new pricing plan has grown into a $4 billion business.[48]

XOJET: A BUSINESS JET COMPANY
FOCUSED ON INNOVATIVE PRICING

Sometimes a mix of pricing strategies can be blended together to create a compelling business strategy. CEO Paul Touw and a fellow pricing devotee, Peter Fuchs, are doing this at XOJET, a business jet services provider based in northern California.

Paul is a data-driven entrepreneur with a single mission: executing new business ideas. When I asked why he entered the private aircraft business, he responded: "The aviation industry doesn't tend to think outside of the box; everyone's following the same path. I knew there was room to be different."[49] Of all of the opportunities to focus on in the aviation industry, Paul chose to innovate on pricing.

The concept of interval ownership has revolutionized the private jet industry. Interval jet ownership involves organizing people who can't justify owning an entire airplane and selling them fractional interests. Shareholders aren't tied to flying on one specific jet; instead they have access to the combined fleet. This pricing concept created a boon for jet manufacturers, opening the opportunity to enjoy the benefits of private jet ownership to a larger group of customers. After all, only a select few can afford (or need) a dedicated jet and its associated expenses such as full-time pilots and crew.

But as Peter, XOJET's vice president of product strategy, explained to me, "There are many problems with the typical fractional jet pricing model."[50] One such problem is the type of low-volume customers attracted to interval ownership. These customers tend to be located in remote areas and fly during peak times. Remote customers, those flying between low traffic cities like Bozeman, Montana and Salt Lake City, usually incur deadhead (no revenue) aircraft positioning costs. An aircraft may have to be flown (without passengers) from Seattle to Bozeman (for the pick up) and then to Las Vegas (after drop-off) for its next revenue bearing flight. Low-volume owners are also apt to fly during peak times like holidays to swank ski resorts for New Years Eve. Interval jet companies incur significant expenses to charter extra aircraft during periods of high demand to satisfy its owners' travel needs.

Another challenge that fractional jet companies face is their ownership programs encompass a wide variety of jets. NetJets, the world's largest interval jet company, sells fractional interests in fifteen different aircraft types. So while a jet and crew may be well-positioned to pick up another owner, if it's the wrong aircraft type, it may not be used. This drawback from operating a diverse aircraft fleet, coupled with the adverse selection issues of unprofitable interval jet customers, creates inefficiencies.

With these problems in mind, Paul and his team brainstormed a solution: XOJET. To minimize adverse-selection customer issues, XOJET caters to high-volume customers (those who fly at least a hundred hours a year). These flyers are often the most profitable, as they travel between highly trafficked destinations, thereby minimizing profit-draining deadhead flights. These travelers are less likely to fly during peak holiday periods, so focusing on this segment eliminates costly charter rentals during those periods. Serving high-volume customers also makes sense because it's easier to schedule aircraft. Having four 200-hour customers per jet instead of thirty-two 25-hour customers reduces travel overlaps that require expensive charters from outside companies. And finally, the company only operates two of the most popular aircraft models preferred by their target customers.

There are two ways to fly with XOJET. First, you can contract for one hundred or more hours of flight time per year. Second, if an aircraft is available, it can be chartered on a per-flight basis. These two pricing plans allow XOJET to operate a cost-efficient model that Paul terms "dynamic allocation"—the ability to increase capacity during peak times and reduce it during off-peak periods. The company has enough jets to guarantee that a company-owned plane will be available to serve its high-volume contract customers. This is a real benefit to flyers, as there are quality control concerns if outside (non-XOJET) charters have to be used to satisfy high demand. To make good on this guarantee, XOJET often has excess capacity, which it then fills with charter flights. When demand from its contract customers is high, charter flights are curtailed. Conversely, when contract customer demand is low, the charter flight "faucet" is opened.

The benefit of offering these two pricing plans is high efficiency. XOJET's planes fly an average 1,240 hours per year, of which a remarkable 97% are revenue-bearing.[51] As a result, the price to customers of flying is 20 to 40% lower than with rival services. XOJET also offers its contract customers an option to benefit from the tax depreciation advantages of owning a jet. The company is thriving: 2007 revenues were up 80%, customers purchasing more than 100 hours increased by 500% (the average contract was for more than 150 hours per year), and its fleet is increasing from 20 to 127 planes. In addition, the company completed one of the largest debt and equity deals of 2008, a sign of confidence in a challenging capital market.

XOJET is a prime example of how an innovative pricing plan can serve as the backbone of a "disruptive" business model. XOJET's focus on leasing to high-volume customers coupled with offering one-off charters allows it to attract new customers, provide better service, and save its clients money.

When I asked Peter to elaborate on the lessons that he had learned from this experience, his response reinforced the key theme of this book: "One size"—that is, one price—"does *not* fit all."

EXAMPLE: PICK-A-PLAN—ORANGE MYPOD

Returning to the myPod example, in addition to setting a value-based price, to meet the needs of potential customers Orange can offer new pricing plans such as (1) short-term leases, (2) the option to trade in an old myPod for a new one (for customers anxious to own the latest myPod), and (3) a value bundle that includes unlimited music downloads.

PICK-A-PLAN AND REAPING A FINANCIAL WINDFALL

The power of pick-a-plan strategies comes from the ability to sell products to new segments of customers by better meeting their pricing needs. As Terminix is experiencing, pick-a-plan tactics can generate new customers in a slow-growth industry. And as XOJET is demonstrating, a combination of pricing plans can be the basis for a new business. Implementing new pricing plans, like those created by Steve Good at Terminix and Paul Touw at XOJET, can generate blockbuster growth and, as a result, produce a pricing windfall.

KEY TAKEAWAYS

PICK-A-PLAN

- Many customers are interested in a product but refrain from purchasing because the pricing strategy doesn't work for them. Pick-a-plan involves offering new pricing plans that activate these dormant customers.
- Pick-a-plan pricing tactics are classified into four core groups: (1) ownership alternatives, (2) uncertain value, (3) price assurance, and (4) financial and other constraints.
- Ownership alternatives recognize that some customers don't want to own product. However, they may be interested in other options to use it, including:

  - Interval ownership: divide a whole product into smaller ownership units and sell incremental units individually.
  - Leasing: sell the right to use a product for a fixed period.
  - Rental: allow usage of a product for a period shorter than leases.
  - Netflix model: offer a type of rental that involves paying a fixed monthly price for access to a vast catalog and a set number of product rentals with exchange privileges.

- Uncertain-value pricing tactics reduce the risk associated with a product. Risk reduction tactics include:

  - Success fees: usually involve a base price plus a bonus if a key success metric is achieved.
  - Licensing: allow outside parties to use intellectual property (trademarks, patents, or technology) for financial compensation tied to the value of its contribution.
  - Auctions: establish value by accepting bids for a product and selling to the highest bidder at the end of a fixed period.
  - Future purchase options: the right, but not the obligation, to purchase a product in the future.

- Price certainty is targeted to customers who prefer to reduce or eliminate swings in prices. Key pricing tactics that reduce this kind of uncertainty are:

  - Flat rate: offer a fixed fee to undertake a project (in lieu of billing by the hour).
  - Peace-of-mind guarantee: fix a product's price for a given period.
  - All-you-can-eat: offer one price for unlimited usage.
  - Two-part high/low pricing: charge an up-front price (membership, which is the primary source of profit) and then set lower-than-general-market variable prices.

- Plans that address financing and other constraints recognize that consumers may need to spread out payments or may not meet (or need) the requirements of current pricing plans. Pricing tactics to overcome these issues include:

- Financing: allow customers to make payments over time.
- Job-loss protection: offer refunds or payments if a customer becomes unemployed.
- Layaway: allow customers to pay in installments and receive merchandise only when full payment is made.
- Prepaid plans: permit customers to pay in advance and then draw down this credit with usage.

3

Versioning

I HAVE JUST THE RIGHT PRODUCT FOR YOU

A slight tweak to a product's characteristics can attract new customers. This is what Terrance Brennan has discovered at Picholine, his restaurant in New York City. Terrance, the chef-proprietor, has built his menu around the principle of offering his customers choices (of product versions) to experience his culinary creations. Customers appreciate this flexibility and have told him that it's "nice to have options."[1]

Starting out as a cook in his father's northern Virginia restaurant, Brennan apprenticed through a series of restaurant jobs and by age twenty-one had risen to the position of executive sous chef at a two-thousand-room Sheraton hotel in Washington, D.C. Seeking his next opportunity, he took a job at the acclaimed Le Cirque in New York City. Later he worked in several three-star Michelin restaurants throughout Europe. Returning to New York in 2003, he opened Picholine.

Chef Brennan's intense and perfectionist personality, reflected in what he describes as his daily challenge of "making the restaurant experience better," has drawn accolades in New York's competitive restaurant environment. Picholine earned three stars (out of four) from the *New York Times* and two stars (out of three) from the Michelin Guide, and it has been nominated for the James Beard Outstanding Restaurant award.

While the cuisine is wonderful, what attracted me (and many customers) to Picholine was the restaurant's variety of pricing alternatives. The range of dining options include:

- Lower-priced bar area
- Two-course pretheater menu served from 5:00 to 6:15 P.M.
- À la carte menu offering set prices for three courses with the option to add more courses
- Two premium chef's tasting menus
- Private eight-person Wine Room
- Larger private dining room for events

On any given night, diners range from budget-minded young couples sampling tapas at the bar to executives hosting dinners in the higher-priced Wine Room, which veteran food critic Ruth Reichl described as "one of the prettiest dining rooms in New York."[2] Reinforcing the role of versioning and its ability to serve new customers, reviewers from the *New York Times*, the *New York Post*, and *New York Magazine* have all noted that the restaurant's new menu versions and pricing structure are aimed at attracting a younger crowd.[3]

Underscoring a key point of versioning, Brennan explained that these versions are not just about price. In his customers' eyes, these versions offer different products and experiences. "If you want to feel like a celebrity," he noted, "order the tasting menu. If you want a delicious meal but don't want to sit for three hours, order à la carte."

The options at Picholine illustrate the two primary benefits of versions: offering financial advantages and meeting specific needs. Pricing options make a product accessible and attractive to consumers with a wider range of incomes. On a tight budget? Dine at the bar or during pretheater hours. When dining on an expense account, order the chef's tasting menu. What's fascinating is that some customers purchase these same options not for financial reasons but instead to meet specific needs. Want to dine before attending the Metropolitan Opera? Try the pretheater special. If you are celebrating an important anniversary, sign up for a multicourse meal that includes selections from the restaurant's more than sixty artisanal cheeses.

As Brennan demonstrates, better pricing is not just about extracting profits from customers; it also involves offering benefits to customers.

VERSIONING

Think about how limited Picholine's business would be if it just offered an à la carte menu. Fewer customers would enjoy Chef Brennan's cuisine, and Picholine would miss out on profits. This is why every company should consider versioning its products. Versioning involves using a core product as a base and adding or subtracting attributes in a manner that serves more customers. This pricing tactic attracts new customers who value a product differently as well as those with unique needs. Companies also benefit from current customers who choose to upgrade to more profitable products (as Southwest Airlines discovered with its Business Select ticket versions).

Versioning can be used to serve and capture profit from customers with different valuations. Returning to the restaurant example, versioning can be thought of as offering a line of early-bird (good), regular (better), and chef's-table (best) products. Customers minding their budgets purchase the early-bird specials, while diners with higher valuations pay more for a chef's-table meal. A company can't thrive financially only by catering to early-bird customers. However, these customers cover the restaurant's variable costs (food), contribute to overhead, and may upgrade to the chef's table in the future. Conversely, generous profits can be earned from customers who pay an additional $50 to sit at the chef's table to sample the latest culinary creations and chat with the chef. Attracting this breadth of customers results in growth (more customers) and profits (overhead contributions from early birds as well as improved margins from those who choose to sit at the chef's table).

Versioning can also be used to offer attributes that serve the unique needs of target customer segments. Consider American Express. The credit card company's core products include good (Green, $95 annually), better (Platinum, $450 yearly), and best (Black, $5,000 initiation plus $2,500 annual fee) credit cards, each with its own unique set of benefits. Amex also offers a variety of need-targeted versions, including co-branded cards that earn frequent-flyer points on airlines and hotel stay points, as well as prepaid gift cards. Do you want to earn cash back on your credit card purchases or have 1% of the value of your purchases placed in a high-yield savings account? If so, American Express has a card that can meet those specific needs.

Versioning enables a company to price for profits and growth by earning higher margins from some customers, as well as attracting new ones by better serving their needs and offering both less expensive and premium options. This chapter presents seventeen pricing tactics that involve creating premium versions, selling stripped-down (basic) models, and offering versions that serve the unique needs of target customers.

Figure 3-1
VERSIONING PRICING TACTICS

PREMIUM	STRIPPED DOWN	UNIQUE CUSTOMER NEEDS
• Higher quality	• Lower quality	• Package size
• Guaranteed access	• More restrictions	• Extended and
• Priority access	• Unbundling (à la carte)	enhanced warranties
• Faster	• Off-peak	• Monthly clubs
• Low deductibles and	• Private label	• Bundling
better coverage	• Higher deductibles and	• Platforms
	lower benefits	• Usage purpose

PREMIUM VERSIONS

Premium versions involve adding superior attributes to a product. There is an opportunity to offer a "best" version for most products. These high-end products generate purchases from current buyers who love a product, new clients attracted to the upgraded attributes, and less price-sensitive customers (a surprisingly large number, actually) who automatically select the best option. Premium versioning tactics include selling higher-quality items, guaranteeing access to a product, making priority access available, creating faster products, and offering low deductibles/better coverage insurance.

Higher Quality

"I want, and am willing to pay for, the best."

Higher-quality versions involve enhancing a product's value with new attributes. Offering a better version benefits companies in two primary ways. First, investments in current products can be leveraged and extended into a more upscale market. Ralph Lauren's lines of clothing range from its popular everyday wear with the Polo insignia to its premium Purple Label collection. By creating this high-end version, Ralph Lauren's clothing now competes with exclusive brands such as Gucci and Armani. Second, enhanced products can profit from devoted customers who want and are willing to pay for more. A better version enables these devotees to trade up to the premium version. Diehard fans of the Disney film *The Lion King* bypass the $10.95 DVD in favor of purchasing the $108.89 Disney Special Platinum Edition Collector's Gift Set version.

Because of these profit and customer loyalty benefits, many companies offer higher-quality versions:

- Starbucks sells drip coffee *and,* for roughly a 33% premium, individually brewed premium coffee from its proprietary Clover machines, which the Seattle-based chain pledges "deliver a one-of-a-kind brewed coffee experience that fits with Starbucks' history of coffee expertise."[4]

- Toro manufactures Recycler home lawnmowers that are "more affordable than ever," as well as Super Recycler mowers, priced about 50% higher, which have "premium, high performance features that will keep your lawn beautifully manicured for years to come."[5]

- M&M's offers a regular version for as low as $1.40 for six ounces, as well as premium versions that are priced at $3.99 for a six-ounce package.[6]

- Ralph Lauren sells white dress shirts ranging from $79.50 (Polo Ralph Lauren brand) to $365 (Purple Label).

- Service firms such as accounting or law firms have employees ranging from freshly minted associates to marquee-name senior partners. Routine work can be completed by lower-priced associates, while "big-thinking" challenges can be handled by more experienced senior partners.

Guaranteed Access

"I want a guarantee that I'll be able to buy your service or product."

Paying for guaranteed access ensures that a product or service is available when needed. Do you want to ensure getting tickets to a popular movie on Saturday night? For a $1 convenience charge (approximately a 10% premium on a movie ticket), Fandango will sell you a movie ticket in advance from the comfort of your home.

It's always stressful parking at Boston's Logan Airport. On busy travel days and school vacation weeks, the entire parking lot may be full. The anxiety of searching for a parking spot (and perhaps not finding one) adds to the stresses of flying. Logan Airport's PASSport Gold premium parking program adds value by solving these inconveniences. For an annual fee of $100 ($200 for the first year) and a 20% premium over daily parking rates, PASSport Gold members are guaranteed a parking space. To accommodate these customers, cordoned-off areas that are located close to terminals are reserved for premium parkers. Cars are valet-parked if a space is not available.[7]

Priority Access

"I'm willing to pay more to go to the head of the line."

A surefire way to frustrate customers is to make them wait in line. Selling priority access involves charging more to bypass waiting for a product or service. After a long flight, it's an unpleasant gamble whether the rental car line will be short or a forty-five-minute ordeal. Major car rental companies have recognized this concern and have programs (for a fee, or complimentary to frequent renters) that allow customers to avoid lines and go directly to their cars.

And while offering priority access can entice current customers to trade up, companies often use this strategy to attract new customers. Long waits for popular rides are the biggest complaint of guests at amusement parks.[8] To address this issue, many amusement parks have created no-wait admission ticket versions. The regular admission price to Six Flags amusement park in Chicago is $54.99. However, an additional $245 anoints you a VIP, allowing you to go to the head of lines. This VIP package was created after Six Flags' research found that new customers were interested in visiting the park but were seeking a more private experience to avoid large crowds.[9] Similarly, lines to enter the observation deck of the Empire State Building in New York can be as long as ninety minutes. For double the regular price, customers can purchase express admission that guarantees a wait time of less than twenty minutes. This option was created to serve customers who were walking away at the sight of long lines.[10]

The concept of priority access is akin to rush service. Customers asking for same-day service for dry cleaning or delivery are revealing a willingness to pay more (a premium). A request for a product "as soon as possible" is a value-based opportunity to increase prices.

Faster Product

"I value speed."

A faster version of a product captures the value customers place on saving time. Analysts predict that in the next generation of computers, bragging rights will go to manufacturers of machines that boot up faster.[11] Microsoft claims that a very good system is one that boots up in fifteen seconds or less.

How much would you pay to shave forty-five minutes off your travel time between Boston to New York? On this route, Amtrak, the commercial rail carrier, offers high-speed Acela service (travel time: three hours and 30 minutes; price: $124), as well as regular train service (travel time: four hours and 15 minutes; price: $89). So would you pay the extra $35 to save forty-five minutes? Apparently travelers do value speed, because close to 11 million passengers annually opt to take the Acela high-speed service that connects major cities in the Northeast.[12]

Low Deductibles and Better Coverage

"I prefer an insurance policy with low deductibles and comprehensive coverage."

Consumers concerned with risk and the potential of having to make a high payment, in the event of a loss, value insurance policies with low deductibles and better coverage. Allstate insurance has been successful in attracting customers to its top-of-the-line Your Choice auto insurance program. For a higher annual fee, Your Choice insurance provides benefits such as accident forgiveness (rates don't increase after a first accident) and new car replacement (in the event of a total loss, Allstate will purchase a new car instead of paying out the depreciated value). Drivers have embraced this new insurance program and are signing up at a rate of 100,000 new policies per month.[13]

STRIPPED-DOWN VERSIONS

Designing a basic version involves trimming a product's attributes and reducing its price. These versions attract customers who would not normally purchase, but are willing to accept, fewer attributes in exchange for a discount. Stripped-down versions include offering lower quality, imposing restrictions, unbundling a product, setting off-peak discounts, manufacturing private-label products, and selling insurance with higher deductibles and lower benefits.

Lower Quality

"I'm interested in your product; do you have a discounted version with fewer features?"

Offering a lower-quality version of a product involves reducing the number of attributes to decrease the price. Many companies with well-established brands profit from this opportunity to serve new, more price-sensitive customers, with discounted lower quality versions:

- Wolfgang Puck's Cut steakhouse sells Japanese Wagyu steak for $20 an ounce, as well as USDA prime steak for $2 an ounce.
- For a one-pound package, the U.S. Postal Service prices Express Mail overnight guaranteed at $23.40, but seven-day media mail is just $2.23.

- For $144.95 per month, Verizon provides premium fiber-optic Internet service (which it claims is up to ten times faster than cable Internet service), and they also offer a much slower DSL service for $19.99 per month.
- The Los Angeles Lakers sell individual game tickets for as much as $2,500 (courtside) and as little as $10 (located at the top of the arena).
- Sears sells a spectrum of auto batteries that range from its Diehard Platinum for $189.99 (four-year warranty) to a $69.99 Diehard North (eighteen-month warranty).

Interested in the differences between car batteries, I asked the owner of a local repair garage, Ray Magliozzi ("Clack" of National Public Radio's *Car Talk*), for his opinion. "You should buy whatever battery we sell," he joked.[14] He then went on to discuss the cold cranking amps of particular batteries. The colder your winter is, the more cold cranking amps you need. "You don't need to worry as much about cranking amps in South Carolina, but the harsh winters in Massachusetts require more amps," Ray pointed out.

The key point is that most brand-name products have the opportunity to sell to more customers by providing a range of options.

More Restrictions

"I am willing to accept more restrictions for a discount."

Customers can be segmented by attaching more restrictions or conditions to a discount. Those willing to abide by rules receive a discount. Higher-priced options offer more freedoms.

The variety of ticket prices sold by an airline can be considered, in essence, a line of product versions. Lower-priced tickets, targeted to leisure passengers, come with restrictions such as advance purchase requirements and fees for making changes. Higher fares, generally sold to business travelers, have no restrictions: book and fly at any time, and there are no charges for making ticket changes. Given this pricing practice, it's common for a traveler who paid $2,000 for his or her ticket to be sitting next to someone who paid only $200.

I was surprised to discover how many airline travelers use discount fares. The Bureau of Labor Statistics (BLS) analyzes airfares to compute the U.S. Consumer Price Index. Sampling from actual airfare pricing data, the BLS has determined that 94% of airline tickets are discounted coach, 4% are full-fare coach, and 2% are first class.[15] This large percentage of discounts reveals the importance of versioning to the airline industry.

Unbundling

"I'm only interested in buying a part of your product."

Unbundling (à la carte) is the practice of allowing customers to purchase parts of a product instead of the whole. The music industry has unbundled CDs and is now aggressively selling digital singles. The chance to purchase individual tracks has resonated with music fans: a total of 844.2 million digital tracks were sold in 2008 (up 45% from the previous year).[16]

The airline industry is unbundling the flying experience. Paying one price used to cover virtually all aspects of flying. Now, due to unbundling, paying for an airline ticket is just the starting point. Extra fees are imposed for making reservations by phone (as opposed to the Internet), meals, pillows/blankets, checking luggage, and even redeeming frequent-flyer mileage. This unbundling trend emerged for two reasons. First, airlines with the best fares receive preferential positioning (highlighted as the "lowest fare" for a search) on travel websites such as Orbitz and at travel agencies. This provides airlines with an incentive to list the lowest possible prices (additional charges are noted with asterisks or in small print). Also, offering options allows customers to choose the price that works best for them. A price-sensitive customer can save more than $75 per round trip by making reservations online, not checking luggage, and skipping onboard meals.

One condition for approving the merger between satellite radio companies Sirius and XM was that the combined company offer à la carte pricing. Prior to the merger, both companies offered a one-price strategy that allowed access to all of their programming. Now they sell lower-price options such as family, music, and news/talk radio packages that are targeted toward specific customer segments. More unbundling may be forthcoming in the entertainment industry. The Federal Communications Commission is interested in requiring cable television companies to allow consumers to select their channels à la carte style in addition to the bundles that are currently offered.

Off-Peak Pricing

"For a discount, I'd purchase during off-peak times."

Off-peak pricing involves setting discount prices to attract more customers during periods of low demand. This strategy is commonly used for fixed-capacity products including hotels, power companies, toll roads, bridges, and even bowling alleys.

Sonic is a fast-food chain differentiated in part by the variety of non-alcoholic drinks that it sells. This selection includes slushies, limeade, soft drinks, teas, smoothies, and coffees that can be mixed together into over 168,000 different combinations. To spur sales during off-peak times, Sonic started a 50% off Happy Hour between 2:00 and 4:00 P.M. on its drinks. After this initiative began, the restaurant's quarterly profits increased by 49% and its same-store sales grew by 3.2%. Sonic singled out this Happy Hour promotion as a "strong contributor" to its financial results.[17] After businesses (such as restaurants) cover their high fixed costs, additional revenues have generous profit margins. As a result, discount promotions that push revenues above the fixed-cost threshold can have a big impact on profits as well as stimulate additional full-price purchases.

Off-peak pricing is becoming a popular strategy for electric utility companies to use in their home consumer markets. To avoid the cost of building new power plants to meet periods of high demand, utility companies are offering financial incentives for consumers to reduce their consumption during these potential capacity breaking times. Baltimore Gas and Electric (BGE) is running an off-peak, peak, and critical peak price pilot program that involves charging 9 cents per kilowatt-hour (enough energy to power a 100-watt lightbulb for ten hours) during off-peak times, 14 cents per kilowatt-hour during peak times (2:00 to 7:00 P.M. on weekdays), and $1.30 per kilowatt-hour during times deemed to be "critical peak" (periods when energy demand is expected to exceed capacity). When demand could exceed supply, customers are notified of impending high prices. Customers can then evaluate whether it's worth using large amounts of energy to do laundry or turn on their air conditioner.[18]

Off-peak pricing isn't always implemented to shift demand from peak to off-peak periods. Many times off-peak discount prices are used to serve customers who otherwise wouldn't purchase at all. Tactics such as half-price tennis on Tuesdays and low-season Caribbean summer specials are intended to use discount prices as an incentive for new customers to utilize capacity that otherwise would go unsold.

Private Label

"If the price is right, I'll buy your private-label product."

In the private-label strategy, a manufacturer sells its product (or a lower-quality version) not with its brand name on the label but under a retailer's name. This is a growing market within the food industry. Private-label products hold an 11.4% market share of total household and personal care product sales, with major retailers such as Trader Joe's and Wegmans creating their own private-label brands.[19]

Many well-known companies produce private-label products in the same plants using the identical or similar ingredients as they do for their branded products. Companies do so to reap efficiencies of keeping their plants working. A senior executive at Chicken of the Sea claims that private-label products are less profitable but maximize cannery production (keeping employees busy and reducing waste from unused product).[20] The Private Label Manufacturers Association estimates that 65% of all food and beverage companies, including Sara Lee, Hormel, Birds Eye, and Del Monte, are involved in private-label manufacturing.[21]

Of course, companies with strong brands aren't pleased if it becomes known that they also supply private-label products. It devalues a brand. Macallan is an exceptional single-malt whisky, and a 750 ml bottle of its eighteen-year-old scotch retails for around $140. Costco started selling a same-sized bottle of eighteen-year-old scotch for $60 under its Kirkland private-label brand. Right below the Kirkland logo are the words "Macallan Distillery." Intrigued, the Wall Street Journal investigated. A Macallan spokesperson admitted that yes, the company produced the Kirkland scotch. Twenty years ago, Macallan had excess supply and sold the surplus to independent bottlers to store and bottle under their own labels. This supply ended up on Costco's shelves.[22]

Private-label versions benefits retailers, consumers, and manufacturers. Well-known retailers such as Whole Foods, Target, and Kroger make more money by leveraging the confidence in their brands to roll out lower-priced private-label products that save their customers money but offer a higher per-unit profit. Manufacturers can extend their customer base without affecting their high-end brands by making private-label versions.

High Deductibles and Lower Benefits

"Can you offer me a lower price in return for lower insurance benefits?"

High deductibles and lower benefits is a strategy that can attract customers seeking more affordable alternatives. With health insurance premiums increasing by 119% between 1999 and 2008 and earnings only rising 34% during this same time period, analyzing the trade-off between premiums and coverage is becoming increasingly necessary in health care. Increasing annual deductibles to $2,000 can reduce monthly premiums by 20 to 35%. The percentage of workers enrolled in plans with a deductible of $1,000 or more increased by 50% in one year (2007 to 2008). Furthermore, more than one in three workers in small businesses covered by health insurance have deductibles that are greater than $1,000.[23]

UNIQUE CUSTOMER NEEDS

Versions can satisfy a specific need of target customers. Adding a new attribute or service to a product (an organic version, for instance) can appeal to new customers. Versions that meet unique customer needs include selling different package sizes, offering extended and enhanced warranties, starting monthly clubs, creating bundles, making products available in different platforms, and using a product for a new purpose.

Package Size

"I'd value a different-size package of your product."

The package size tactic involves offering different package sizes to meet customers' needs. Take regular versus magnum bottles of champagne. The pricing of these different-size bottles defies the general practice that the more you buy, the lower the per-serving price. Morrell & Company in New York City sells Veuve Clicquot Champagne (nonvintage) at $43 for a full bottle (750 ml) and $115 for a magnum (1,500 ml). The magnum price represents a 34% premium over purchasing two regular-size bottles.[24] And while there is a debate over whether wine ages better in a magnum, for nonvintage champagnes at least, the premium seems to capture the celebratory value of showing up at a party with a large champagne bottle.

A trend in the snack food industry is to offer smaller, 100-calorie package versions. These smaller packages target market segments interested in portion control, including dieters and schoolkids who bring their own lunches. From a portion control perspective, most consumers won't count out and pack up the sixteen potato chips that make up a single serving size. However, many prefer smaller prepackaged units that impose single-serving restraint. According to Information Resources, sales of 100-calorie packs increased by 28% in 2006, while the snack food industry as a whole grew by just 3.5%.[25] Additionally, offering these smaller-size products grows sales and is also more profitable. It is estimated that snack-size packages are about 20% more profitable compared to larger sizes.[26]

Extended and Enhanced Warranties

"A premium warranty is important to me when purchasing products."

Selling extended and enhanced warranties interests customers who value the security of knowing that future repairs will be covered and efficiently completed. I always purchase laptop computers from Dell because it is the only laptop manufacturer I know of that sells an enhanced, next-business-day repair warranty. Because their quick and convenient repair commitment is important to me, I don't even consider products from competitors.

Most consumer trade organizations have determined that extended warranties are unnecessary and overpriced. "Almost all of it [the additional premium] will be money down the drain," is the opinion of *Consumer Reports*.[27] It may make financial sense to self-insure, but extended warranties do offer additional value, including eliminating anxiety over unexpectedly high repair bills, guaranteeing next-day service, an immediate exchange for a new product if necessary, and the convenience of not having to shop around for service or worrying about being taken advantage of when a repair is made.

So yes, in actuarial terms, *Consumer Reports* is probably correct. However, value to customers involves more than a financial calculation. With these warranty versions, customers are better off because they can select the level of assurance that works best for them.

The option of a premium warranty draws in new customers and is profitable to sellers. Analysts estimate that extended warranties account for 50% to 100% of the operating profits of electronics retailers such as Best Buy.[28]

Monthly Clubs

"I'm interested in receiving a new product every month."

A popular selling technique for products ranging from fruits to bacon is using a monthly club (product-of-the-month). This versioning tactic involves sending a new product to subscribers every month. The value of this versioning tactic to consumers includes offering editorial guidance (this is the "best" or the "next big thing") and the convenience of regular shipments. In turn, companies benefit by attracting loyal customers who are typically less price-sensitive. Monthly clubs serve aficionados and those shopping for gifts.

In spite of intense competition from Internet retailers of books and music, recent statistics show that 20 million Americans belong to a book or record club.[29] Interestingly, the key demographic for these clubs is women in their forties. Reinforcing the value of expert judgment, one member explained to the *Wall Street Journal* the reason for joining a book club: "What you're getting is editorial selectivity. They cut through a lot of titles and present the ones you should consider."[30]

Bundling

"I'd like the convenience of purchasing your product in tandem with another product."

Bundling is the pricing strategy of offering multiple products together to meet a specific customer need. Convenience is a big reason why consumers purchase a bundle. Bundling is *the* trend in the telecommunications industry: one purchase covers services such as landline, long distance, wireless, Internet, and television. Quest Communications reports that nearly 60% of its customers purchase a bundle that includes three or more of its services.[31] Telecommunications companies find that these bundles increase loyalty (it's harder to switch providers) and allows them to sell more services to each of their accounts.[32]

Bundling is commonly used in the automobile industry. The Ford Mustang has 140 different options, such as a 4.0 liter V-6 engine with stainless-steel single exhaust or a 4.6 liter V-8 engine with dual exhaust. To simplify the decision-making process, Ford offers bundled versions of its Mustang that range from the $20,400 Mustang V-6 coupe to the $34,000 Mustang Premium convertible.[33] Similarly, to help its customers make decisions about the many components associated with brake repair (pad/shoe warranty, rotor/drum services, brake fluid flush/fill, caliper slide service, and so on), the car repair chain Meineke offers three easy-to-purchase bundle options: "basic," "preferred," and "supreme."

Platforms

"I'm interested in your product but want to enjoy it on a different platform."

Offering the same basic product on different platforms (avenues to use a product) attracts new customers. Consider the multiple platforms that books are sold on. In addition to print, book content is sold in digital, audio, and video formats.

Usage Purpose

"I'm interested in using your product for a different purpose."

Usage purpose versioning involves modifying a product so it can be used for a new reason. A change in a product can open up new markets. Examples of usage purpose versioning include:

- While pickles are generally consumed as a side dish for sand-wiches, Vlasic decided that more people should put pickles *in* their sandwiches. The company found that only 3% of the 35 billion sandwiches consumed in U.S. homes have pickles in them. To target the 33.9 billion sandwiches that *could* include pickles, Vlasic created its Stackers product line. Stackers are whole pickles that are thinly sliced lengthwise to fit into sand-wiches. There's high profit in these slices: a 32-ounce jar of Vlasic whole dill pickles sells for $3.49 (11 cents per ounce), while a 16-ounce jar of Stackers dill pickles sells for $2.99 (19 cents per ounce). Stackers were an instant hit with consumers, with first-year sales exceeding $60 million.[34]
- For drugs that have proved successful for humans, pharmaceu-tical companies often create versions for pets. These versions are priced differently, as highlighted by presidential candidate Al Gore at a campaign speech in Tallahassee, Florida. Before an audience of senior citizens, Mr. Gore mentioned that his mother-

in-law paid $108 per month for the arthritis drug Lodine, while the pet version of Lodine (Etogesic) for his fourteen-year-old Labrador retriever was priced at $37.80 per month.[35]

- Many dentists do a good job of pricing to capture the value of their range of services. The gross hourly wage of a dentist (subtracting lab costs but not overhead) can run from $100 (providing exams on patients after a cleaning) to over $1,000 (crowns and dental implants).

- Digital music is also versioned based on its purpose: 99-cent songs for general listening, $1.99 ringback tones (when calling a party with a cell phone, instead of hearing a traditional ringtone, the caller hears snippets of a song), and $2.99 caller ringtones (instead of a standard ring indicating that someone is calling, cell phones play a song).

B.B.'S BUNDLE: 1 + 1 = 3

As bluesman B.B. King has discovered, bundling a product with others can yield significant growth in value and thus profits. In the concert industry, the axiom for bundling two acts together is 1 + 1 = 3: the number of people attending a bundled concert with two acts should be more than the sum of those who would attend each act separately.

Hailed as the reigning king of the blues, B.B. King grew up as a poor sharecropper in Mississippi. At age twenty he went to Memphis, guitar in hand and $2.50 in his pocket, to pursue a career in music. Mr. King's determination to constantly tour to play his music before live audiences is unrivaled. In 1956 he played 342 one-night concerts, and he regularly performed more than 200 concerts annually until he turned eighty years old. B.B.'s efforts have been rewarded with great success. He has sold over 40 million records, won ten Grammy awards, received five honorary doctorates, and was awarded the Presidential Medal of Freedom, the nation's highest civilian award.[36]

And while I'm a fan of his music, B.B. King is a strategy master bundler. Since 2000, he has toured with his band for most of the year. During the summers, he and his band headline the traveling B.B. King Blues Festival, which includes two or three other artists on the bill. He creates a blues bundle. This four-hour blues music festival works its way across the United States and plays venues that are considerably larger than those that King uses when it's just him and his band.

The high attendance and financial rewards of this concert bundle illustrate the 1 + 1 = 3 principle. In March 2007, B.B. King and his band played at the Thomas Wolfe Auditorium in Asheville, North Carolina. With ticket prices ranging from $39.50 to $49.50, 1,963 people attended this solo show, which grossed $91,369 in revenue. However, in September of that same year, his Blues Festival (which included Al Green and Etta James) played at the Red Rocks Amphitheater in Morrison, Colorado. With tickets priced from $49 to $89, 8,634 people attended the show for a total gross of $574,888. The Blues Festival attracts both a larger audience and segments that are willing to pay higher ticket prices, a double win for King. For dates involving just him and his band, Mr. King averaged an attendance of 1,877 ($109,198 in revenue), while his Blues Festivals averaged 5,391 attendees ($290,415 in revenue).[37] By creating a bundle that includes a few lesser-known acts, Mr. King almost triples his attendance and revenue. The result: new profits from the 1 + 1 = 3 value creation.

To better understand bundling in the concert industry, I turned to Marc Geiger, an executive vice president at William Morris Endeavor Entertainment. Marc is known for bringing solid business discipline to the music industry, which he characterizes as a "cowboy industry."[38] "Bundling is pretty straightforward," Marc explained. The reasons why musicians such as B.B. King create concert bundles include:

- Provide more value to consumers
- Allow a band to "scale" (play in front of more people than they otherwise would), resulting in more profits, exposure, and ancillary sales

- Fulfill an artist's dream or embody a concept (the Lilith Fair, for instance, was a traveling concert tour that featured female musicians)

Because he is an "oversupplier" (someone who tours a lot), King needs to offer fans a new product to purchase. Summing up the new product angle of creating a bundle, Marc pointed out, "And this is what the B.B. King Blues Festival does. If you like blues, this is the only way to get a lot of blues in one fell swoop."

Expanding our discussion beyond bundling to concert ticket pricing, Marc summed up the changes that he believes need to be made: "It's all about choice." He advocates offering several different price levels for a concert that consumers can select from: "It's stupid not to. Events that don't offer multiple prices are cutting off consumers." The theme that pricing experts such as Marc Geiger consistently come back to is the concept of giving customers pricing choices.

Versioning implicitly results in different prices for different customers. Stripped-down versions offer discounts, while more margin is derived from premium versions. Increased profits from these higher margins and new customers (attracted to various versions) are a key component of every company's pricing windfall campaign.

VERSIONING: ORANGE MYPOD PLAYER

Returning to the ongoing myPod example, Orange can offer higher- and lower-priced product versions. Both a discounted, stripped-down Shuffle (no video screen) and a premium priced, full-featured Touch (wide video screen, Wi-Fi Web-enabled) can be added to the product line.

VERSIONING AND A PRICING WINDFALL

Think of versioning as a bridge between pick-a-plan and differential pricing strategies. Just as pick-a-plan attracts customers with a new pricing plan, versioning opens the door for new clients by changing product attributes. And similar to differential pricing, versioning extracts different margins from different customers. Price-sensitive customers can purchase the low-quality version, while those less concerned with their budgets can buy the profit-packed premium version. These profit- and growth-generating benefits are integral to achieving a financial windfall.

KEY TAKEAWAYS

VERSIONING

- A few minor modifications can attract new customers or entice existing buyers to trade up to products that earn higher profits, as well as appeal to customers with unique needs and lower product valuations.
- Versioning tactics are classified into three core groups: (1) premium attributes, (2) stripped-down, basic products, and (3) unique customer needs.
- Premium attributes involve adding additional features to a product and charging a higher price. Categories of premium attributes include:

  - Higher quality: add attributes that improve a product's overall value.
  - Guaranteed access: ensure availability.

- Priority access: allow customers to avoid waiting.
- Faster product: increase speed.
- Low deductibles and better coverage: offer more comprehensive insurance.

- Stripping down involves reducing the number of attributes attached to a product and discounting the price. Tactics include:

  - Lower quality: decrease attributes.
  - More restrictions: add conditions to using a product.
  - Unbundling (à la carte): sell parts of a product.
  - Off-peak: offer discounts to reduce peak demand, as well as stimulate demand during times of excess capacity.
  - Private label: supply a product under the retailer's name, not a big brand name.
  - High deductibles and lower benefits: reduce coverage insurance and offer a lower cost.

- Unique customer needs involve adding attributes designed to attract key target customers. Tactics that enable products to reach new customers include:

  - Package size: meet specific needs with different sizes.
  - Extended and enhanced warranties: offer better coverage of defects or accidents.
  - Monthly clubs: send a new product monthly.
  - Bundling: add a service or product.
  - Platforms: allow a product to be used in a different medium.
  - Usage purpose: use a product in a different manner.

4

Differential Pricing

MORE PRICES ATTRACT MORE CUSTOMERS

Offering a range of prices for the same product can lead to increased sales and profits by targeting unique customers. This pricing strategy, differential pricing, is commonly practiced in the hotel industry. Consider the variety of prices for the lowest room type (deluxe) on the same dates at the Omni Berkshire hotel in New York City.[1] A nightly rate of $136 was reportedly sold on Priceline.com.[2] New York City Luxury Hotels, a hotel-room selling agent, put forth two prices: $231 (nonrefundable) and $257 (cancelable). Omni gave rates of $214 (nonrefundable rate for American Express cardholders), $257.40 (fully cancelable for members of the American Automobile Association as well as for senior citizens), $267 (for government employees), $277 (Entertainment Card discount), and $285 (standard price). Finally, Easy-to-Book, an online hotel reservations company, listed a rate of $358.80. Fifteen minutes of research yielded prices ranging from $136 to $358.80 per night for the same hotel.

"It's common for a full-service hotel to offer as many as five hundred possible room rates," Bjorn Hanson, Ph.D., a professor at New York University, told me. "This works out to twenty rates for each of its primary room types"—low-, middle-, and high-floor rooms, standard, deluxe, corner, suites, and so on.[3] Eight of the most common strategies responsible for this array of prices include:

- *Yield management.* Based on historical data, hotels map out how many bookings should be made in advance of a specific night (sixty days before the target night booking occupancy should be at 50%). If bookings are ahead of schedule, room prices are raised. However, rates are cut if reservations are below target.

- *Merchant model.* In return for large-volume discounts, travel agencies such as Expedia contract for a set number of rooms annually, which they then resell. If this allotment is not fully resold, they still have to pay for the unused rooms.

- *Volume discounts.* Companies are granted discounts in return for a pledge to purchase an annual minimum number of rooms. While there's usually no penalty if the agreed-upon minimum isn't met, the next year's negotiations will be tougher.

- *Marketing.* In return for endorsements and features in marketing materials, hotels grant discounts to members of groups such as AAA, Sam's Club, and AARP.

- *Bundle.* A discount tactic to target leisure travelers involves selling bundles that include airline tickets and hotels. Some hotels offer lower prices to travel agencies and airlines if their rooms are sold as part of a bundle (which also includes airfare). As a result, rooms that are booked individually are priced higher relative to those purchased in a bundle. Why should this booking distinction lead to different prices? Leisure vacationers, considered to be relatively price-sensitive, tend to book bundles, while travelers on corporate expense accounts usually have their travel agent book each component of their travel separately. Bundles identify and reduce prices to customers with lower valuations.

- *Opaque travel agencies.* Travel agencies such as Priceline and Hotwire that don't advertise discount prices for specific hotels are considered to be "opaque." At these websites, travelers bid (or at Hotwire are offered a price) for an unnamed hotel that meets a traveler's needs (one- to five-star quality level, city, general area of city). A bidder may seek a four-star hotel in the eastern section of midtown Manhattan, for example. The name of the hotel is privately revealed to the bidder only after an acceptable (and nonrefundable) price for the stay is charged to the customer's credit card. Since discounted rates for a specific hotel are not made public, a hotel's brand is not damaged. Opaque travel agencies are good "back-door" outlets to generate revenue from capacity that would otherwise go unused.
- *Conference rates.* Group attendees (weddings, conferences) receive lower rates when purchasing accompanying services such as catering and meeting rooms.
- *Negotiation.* Bjorn confirmed that rates can be negotiated by calling a hotel directly (not a chain's 800 number) to speak with its in-house reservations department. Calling close to an arrival day and demurring that the offered rate is too high may result in a lower price. He explained, "If bookings are lower than expected, reservation managers prefer to give discreet, as opposed to publicly announced, discounts."

Out of curiosity, I asked Bjorn for tips on how price-sensitive travelers can lock in the best rates at a hotel. His advice centered on conducting research, negotiating with hotels, and being persistent.

- *Research.* Find the lowest rate by checking the hotel's website, merchant agents (Expedia, for example), and offers in newspaper ads for discount travel agencies such as Liberty Travel.
- *Negotiate.* Call the hotel directly, mention the best rate found

from research, and ask the reservation agent if he or she can extend a better deal (discount or bundle with extras). Also inquire if a lower price is available for a different arrival date. Book the lowest rate (found from research or the hotel) that can be canceled.

- *Persistence.* As the date of arrival approaches, continue researching and call the hotel to renegotiate when necessary.

As Bjorn highlighted, differential pricing is a profitable strategy that reaps higher margins from some customers, attracts price-sensitive customers with discounts, and helps businesses market their products. These benefits are not limited to just hotels. There are many reasons and tactics for every company to implement differential pricing for its products.

DIFFERENTIAL PRICING

Since some customers are willing to pay more than others, companies that offer just one price per product end up in a trap that I call a pricing catch-22. By this I mean that no matter what price is set, there are missed profit opportunities. Some customers who bought would have paid a higher price, while more would have purchased had the price been lower. Companies that set only a single price miss out on higher margins as well as additional sales.

It would be optimal for sellers if customers simply announced the highest amount they would pay for a product and then purchased at that price. While this is an unrealistic hope, this chapter discusses differential pricing techniques that produce similar benefits. These tactics identify the value customers place on a product and then set that price. Buyers with lower valuations receive discounts, while those willing to spend more are charged higher prices. Differential pricing tactics are generally considered to be fair because customers know about these

Figure 4-1

DIFFERENTIAL PRICING TACTICS

HURDLES	CUSTOMER CHARACTERISTICS	SELLING CHARACTERISTICS	SELLING TECHNIQUES
• Rebate • Sales • Coupons • Price match guarantee • Distribution • Time in sales cycle	• Geography • Readily identifiable traits • Club affiliation • Customer history	• Quantity • Mixed bundling • Different next best alternatives	• Negotiation • Two part: razor/razor-blade pricing • Metering • Dynamic pricing

different prices and select the one that works best for them. New cars are typically priced higher at the beginning of a model year and discounted at the end of the year. Customers who want to be among the first to own a new model choose to pay a premium, while others decide to wait for a lower price.

The primary benefit of differential pricing is that discounts are offered to some customers without reducing prices for all buyers. This minimizes cannibalization, which occurs when customers who normally pay full price take advantage of discount opportunities that are not intended for them. This chapter discusses seventeen differential pricing tactics that involve offering discounts based on hurdles, customer characteristics, selling characteristics, and selling techniques. These tactics break a company out of its pricing catch-22 by offering a range of low to high prices that are tailored to their customers' unique valuations.

HURDLES

Creating hurdles is a popular differential pricing tactic because it requires price-sensitive customers to proactively demonstrate that they want a lower price. Patrons who show up at the Magic Mountain amusement park in Los Angeles with an empty Coca-Cola can (to take advantage of the "buy one get one free with any empty can of Coke" admission promotion) are demonstrating that low prices are important to them. Why create hurdles? Many consumers simply don't care about price. Why cut prices for everyone when many are willing to pay full price? Jumping over hurdles identifies price-sensitive customers and reduces the chance of cannibalization. Hurdle tactics include offering rebates, holding sales, distributing coupons, matching prices, basing prices on the type of distribution outlet, and changing prices over time.

Rebates

"I am willing to fill out forms, mail them, and wait several weeks to get a lower price."

Rebates offer lower prices to those willing to complete paperwork and wait for their money to be sent to them. These discounts lower the final price that can be advertised ("$99.99 after a $20 rebate") but grants the discount only to those who make the redemption efforts. Roughly 400 million rebates, worth $6 billion, are offered annually. Staples and its vendors claim to pay out $3.5 million in rebates every week.[4]

Rebates are attractive to sellers because approximately 50% of eligible customers don't follow through to get their cash back. Because of this, an after-rebate price advertised as 20% off drives sales but ultimately is only a 10% discount if there is a 50% redemption rate. A lower-than-expected redemption rate—50,000 of 104,000 new customers who were eligible for a rebate failed to make a claim—caused TiVo, the DVR (digital video recorder) entertainment company, to surprise Wall Street with better-than-expected financial results. This reduced the company's rebate expenses by $5 million. Even though the rebate was significant ($100), TiVo found that because of the holiday shopping season, many of its customers were too distracted to apply for their discount.[5]

Sales

"If you put it on sale, I'll buy."

Holding periodic sales is a common tactic to discount prices for price-sensitive customers. Those who wait for a sale are rewarded with lower prices. Customers who line up at midnight for after-Thanksgiving sales are revealing their desire for discounts. High interest in discounts on one such day-after-Thanksgiving sale created a ten-mile traffic jam and ninety-minute waits to enter stores at the Pittsburgh-area Prime Outlets Mall.[6] On a typical after-Thanksgiving Friday, 60 million adults shop in the United States and retailers ring up one-day revenues of over $10 billion.[7]

Coupons

"I am willing to be on the lookout for, cut out, organize, carry, and then redeem coupons at a store in return for a discount."

Using coupons is a common and effective strategy to segment lower-from higher-valuation customers. The considerable efforts necessary to redeem coupons identify discount-minded consumers. A recent study conducted by Unilever found that 7.4% of household product sales volume was purchased using coupons.[8]

Price Match Guarantee

"Will you match the discount price that is offered by a rival?"

Retailers including Best Buy offer 110% price match guarantees. If a customer proves that a local retailer offers a lower price on an identical product, Best Buy will match the price plus throw in a bonus discount equal to 10% of the price differential. Similarly, retailers often match rivals' prices and coupons at the time of sale.[9] If a customer makes the effort to cut out a rival's sales page (or coupon) and bring it to a store, that customer cares about price. A price-matching policy garners additional sales by discreetly offering lower prices to price-sensitive customers.

Distribution

"I'm willing to trade convenience for a discount."

The point of distribution can highlight the value that customers place on a product. A gallon of milk can be more expensive at a twenty-four-hour convenience store compared to a large supermarket. However, consumers who are less price-sensitive are willing to pay a premium for the convenience of late hours, easy access, and proximity to their homes. Conversely, those willing to drive longer distances to outlet malls and search through racks of mixed merchandise reap bargains, on average paying 24% less than at regular retail stores.[10]

Coach believes that outlet stores broaden its products' appeal to a new segment of customers. The leather product maker's research found that its typical full-price shopper is a thirty-five-year-old woman who is single or newly married. In contrast, its average outlet shopper is in her mid-forties, a professional, and a mother of two who values functionality over fad. Additionally, to minimize cannibalization, 75% of the merchandise at its outlet stores is exclusive (not sold at regular retail stores), while the remaining 25% is irregulars or closeouts from retail stores.[11]

Time in Sales Cycle

"I'll wait for a lower price."

Charging different prices over time is a classic differential pricing tactic. Prices vary based on the time in the sales cycle. Prices start off high and are lowered over time to open up the market to new customers. Those who highly value a product will purchase immediately at premium prices, while customers who have lower valuations wait for a discount. Such time-dependent pricing is used for seasonal merchandise, including snow blowers and lawn furniture (high prices at the beginning of the season and lower prices at the end), as well as innovations such as new technology. Within two years of the Apple iPhone's introduction, its price decreased from $599 to $399 to $199 to $99.

This tactic works best when sellers such as Apple can dictate when prices should be lowered. Many times companies are not in this position—competition forces discounting. Prices for innovative products can be pushed down by new competition that offers better value (discounts or superior attributes). Generic drugs provide a better value with prices that are 30% to 80% lower than the original branded product that they replace.[12] When a generic alternative to the prescription sleeping aid drug Ambien entered the market, Ambien's sales dropped from $420 million per quarter to $91 million.[13] Similarly, technology advances reduce the value of existing products. Moore's law, named after Intel cofounder Gordon Moore, states that the number of transmitters on a chip will double every two years.[14] This results in more powerful and cheaper technology. The combination of competition and technology advances explains why prices for big-screen televisions have been dropping by 30% annually.[15]

While customers understand that prices will come down over time, prices can't be cut too quickly or drastically. The "discount heard around the world" occurred on September 5, 2007. Just sixty-eight days after the introduction of the highly anticipated iPhone, Apple cut its price from $599 to $399. Early adopters felt taken advantage of and vocalized their anger to the media. Twenty-four hours later, Apple issued an apology and offered a $100 credit to customers who had paid full price.

Apple's deep discount was too drastic and too fast. Had Apple waited until November, it could have positioned the price cut as "for the holidays." I believe that customers would have understood this explanation and rationalized the premium they had paid as the value of being one of the first to own an iPhone. The fallout from this misstep reveals how important pricing is to a company's brand image.

CUSTOMER CHARACTERISTICS

The characteristics of a customer can reflect their valuation of a product, and thus the price he or she is willing to pay. Since senior citizens are presumed to be price-sensitive and often have more time to search for bargains, many companies offer senior discounts. Differential pricing tactics based on customer characteristics include setting prices according to geography, readily verifiable traits, affiliation with organizations, and customer histories.

Geographic Location

"I'm located in an area that values your product differently."

It's common for a product's value to vary by geographic location. These differences occur because of differing objective and subjective needs, as well as income.

The value of protecting corn crops from rootworms differs by geographic region of the country. Rootworms, members of the beetle family, are a bane to corn farmers. Their larvae feed on corn stalk roots, which disrupt the plant's absorption of water and nutrients. This stunts the growth of corn plants. "Rootworm is the No. 1 pest and No. 1 yield robber we have in growing corn," claimed the president of the National Corn Growers Association.[16] The U.S. Department of Agriculture estimated that corn rootworms cause $1 billion in losses every year and that 30 million out of the 80 million acres of corn grown annually are infested with varying levels of the destructive pest.[17]

Pesticides have traditionally been used to protect against rootworms. To eliminate the negative side effects of pesticides (killing other insects and wildlife, as well as possibly endangering humans), Monsanto developed YieldGard, a genetically engineered strain of corn. This corn contains a gene that produces bacteria that target corn root-worm larvae. Larvae that eat the roots of YieldGard corn die shortly thereafter.

Because corn rootworms are more prevalent in some areas com-pared to others, growers have different valuations for protection. To match its prices with these different valuations, Monsanto divides the United States into seven zones based on the level of insect infestation. YieldGard prices range from $29 to $49 per acre, with higher prices attached to zones with a greater level of corn rootworm infestation.[18] Zone pricing captures profits (from high-intensity areas) and also pro-motes growth (discount prices make YieldGard attractive to purchasers in less infested areas).

What's to stop growers located in high-infestation areas (with pre-mium prices) from purchasing YieldGard seeds in a lower-priced area? Monsanto requires growers to sign a license technology agreement that prohibits transferring the rights to anyone else without written permis-sion from the company.

Readily Verifiable Traits

"I'm a customer who values your product lower than others."

Companies often provide lower prices based on readily verifiable traits. Examples of value-revealing traits include:

- *Age*. The Makena golf course in Maui, Hawaii, discounts its $200 greens fees to $70 for golfers under age 18.
- *Status*. Canadian students are eligible for a Student Price Card, which offers 10–15% off at thousands of retailers and restau-rants.

- *Locals versus out-of-towners.* Vacationers who travel to Orlando, Florida, to visit Universal Studios are generally willing to pay more for admission compared to those who live down the street from the amusement park. To serve and profit from these different segments, Universal Studios offers Florida residents a 25–40% discount, as well as the option to purchase annual unlimited-admission passes.

Club Affiliation

"I saw your product featured in my club newsletter. I am eligible for a club discount."

In exchange for being featured in marketing materials, companies offer discounts to customers affiliated with a club. Members receive discounts by showing their membership card or mentioning a promotional code at the time of purchase.

The American Association of Retired Persons (AARP) has more than 36 million members and is the second-largest nongovernmental organization in the United States, after the Roman Catholic Church.[19] To reach this large audience, many of whom are interested in lower prices, companies offer discounts in exchange for endorsement and marketing benefits. AARP discounts range from 20% off prices at outlet stores to specially negotiated motorcycle insurance rates.

Consider AARP's legal solutions program. AARP's research found that 80% of seniors didn't know how to find an attorney.[20] AARP started a legal program to help its constituency. Lawyers who pass a background check and agree to free initial consultations, fixed prices for standard products (simple will, power of attorney, and so on), and a 20% discount off all other services are put on an approved AARP list. Lawyers benefit from the endorsement of a trusted organization and inclusion in marketing materials. Members take comfort in—as well as discounts from—this seal of approval.

Customer History

"Given my history, I value your product differently than others."

A customer's history can reveal his or her valuation of a product. The insurance industry uses the frequency and size of a customer's past claims to determine their insurance premium. A history of several claims reflects a bigger risk (thus greater cost) for an insurance company, as well as a higher valuation from the applicant (who will receive more payouts). Why not change to a new insurance company to avoid scrutiny of past claims? All insurance companies report claims to the Comprehensive Loss Underwriting Exchange (CLUE) database. Before issuing a new policy, every applicant's CLUE report is checked.

Reviewing a customer's history also helps companies that are not in the insurance industry. A customer's purchasing history reveals if he or she regularly pays full price or only purchases with a discount. This information can help target promotions and prices to specific customers. Actively mining a purchase history database can also identify customers who haven't made their usual purchases (or haven't bought in their regular interval) and stimulate new purchases with a discount.

SELLING CHARACTERISTICS

Changing the selling characteristics associated with a product enables companies to charge different prices. New selling characteristics can segment customers who have different product valuations. These tactics involve offering quantity discounts, creating mixed bundles, and recognizing that customers with different next-best alternatives have different valuations.

Quantity

"Since I'm buying a large amount of your product, will you give me a discount?"

The concept of granting a quantity discount is seemingly axiomatic in pricing. While there are sound reasons to provide quantity discounts, my word of caution is that there are cases when it's not necessary. Sometimes a large-volume order is the equivalent of a customer saying, "Thank you, I love the product!"

The underlying reason to offer quantity discounts is to capitalize on the law of diminishing marginal utility. This fundamental concept of microeconomics translates as, "The more of a product consumed, the less value consumers place on an additional unit." The first day of a family vacation at Disney World is filled with fun and excitement: fresh sights and new adventures. However, by the fifth consecutive day of visiting the theme park, the thrill is waning. Disney incorporates these diminishing valuations into its multiday ticket prices. A single-day pass costs $75. An extra $74 purchases a second consecutive day, and $63 more buys a third day. After day three, prices for an additional day drop drastically: a fourth can be added for $7 and a fifth for only $3.

There are restrictions on these multiday passes: the days must be used consecutively, and passes are nontransferable (a buyer's fingerprint is attached to each pass and checked at entry). These features minimize the downside of quantity discounts: setting a lower price for customers who would have paid more. The consecutive-use clause blocks visitors from saving their extra days to use on a future next trip when they are excited to enjoy the park again (and willing to buy a ticket at full price). Nontransferability prevents passes from being resold in front of the park to new visitors who are willing to pay the full $75 admission price.

I asked Mike, a longtime friend who had purchased five-day admission passes for his family, "How was the fifth day?" "Tiring and boring," he responded, but "worth the extra $3." His response reflects the role of diminishing marginal utility in setting quantity discounts: prices must be structured to entice customers to purchase more than they otherwise would have. Mike's family wouldn't have visited Disney World for a fifth consecutive day had the price not been discounted. And while an additional $3 per person is not a large amount of revenue, it's pure profit. Of course, in this case, the primary reason to provide an incentive to continue visiting the park is to earn additional revenue from meals and other purchases.

Most public transportation systems offer volume discounts to commuters. The New York subway charges $2.25 per ride. To target frequent riders, the New York Transit Authority also sells a thirty-day unlimited-ride pass for as low as $89 and adds a 15% bonus on fare card purchases of more than $8.

Mixed Bundling

"I'd like a price break if I purchase two or more products."

The concept of mixed bundling involves selling products both individually as well as together in bundles. To provide an incentive to purchase, bundles are generally priced lower than the sum of the individual product prices.

Bundles are ubiquitous at fast-food chains. "Value meals" that include a sandwich, fries, and drink are typically priced 15% below the sum of their individual prices. At Burger King, bundled meals represent 51% of total sales.[21] Burger King creates bundles to persuade diners to purchase higher-margin items. "Historically, fries and beverages have a greater penny profit margin than sandwich entrees," reports a Burger King executive.[22]

Figure 4-2 ■ Mixed Bundling Newspapers

	GENERAL NEWS CUSTOMER	BUSINESS CUSTOMER
Amount customer is willing to pay for the *New York Times*	$50	$45
Amount customer is willing to pay for the *Wall Street Journal*	$25	$30
Amount customer is willing to pay for both together	$75	$75

If the *Wall Street Journal* price is $30 and the *New York Times* price is $50, the general news customer buys the *New York Times* and the business customer purchases the *Wall Street Journal*. Total revenue: $80.

If a $75 bundle containing both the *New York Times* and the *Wall Street Journal* is offered, both the business and general news consumers purchase the bundle. Total revenue: $150.

By purchasing the bundle, the general news customer implicitly pays more ($50) for the *New York Times* than the business customer does ($45). The business customer implicitly pays more for the *Wall Street Journal* ($30) than the general news consumer does ($25).

While mixed bundling is a popular pricing strategy, most managers I meet don't understand the full capabilities of this pricing tactic. Many view mixed bundling as offering a quantity discount ("we'll give them a discount if they buy more"), which is one of its capabilities. However, the ability of mixed bundling to sell products to customers with different valuations is often overlooked.

Suppose the *New York Times* and the *Wall Street Journal* sell for $50 and $30 per month, respectively, and that there are only two types of customers, business and general news. The business customer is willing to pay $45 for the *Times* and $30 for the *Journal,* while the general news customer will pay $50 for the *Times* and $25 for the *Journal.*

At the $50 (*Times*) and $30 (*Journal*) individual newspaper prices, the business customer would only buy the *Journal* and the general news customer would only purchase the *Times.* Total revenue would be $80. Now suppose that a bundle of the *Times* and *Journal* is offered for $75 per month. Since the business and general news customers are each willing to pay $75 for the two newspapers, both will purchase the bundle. As a result, total revenue would be $150.

Many managers would view the $75 bundle as a $5 quantity discount to get customers to buy more, but it *isn't* a quantity discount. The reason customers purchase this bundle is because they are implicitly charged different prices. When purchasing the bundle, the business customer is really paying $45 for the *Times*, while the general news customer is paying $50. Conversely, the business customer is paying $30 for the *Journal*, while the general news customer is only paying $25.

Mixed bundling can also be used to target price-sensitive segments, match the competition, and market a combination of products. Families are often considered to be budget-constrained compared to individuals or couples. To target this price-sensitive segment, a pizzeria may offer a discounted meal bundle composed of products that make up a family dinner, such as salad, a large pizza, soda, and dessert. Many times bundles are prevalent in an industry to remain competitive. Since most fast-food restaurants offer discount meal bundles, those that don't offer value bundles are disadvantaged. Finally, a discounted bundle can be used as a marketing tactic to gain customers' attentions. Advertising a 20% discount provides a financial reason for consumers to become aware of and consider purchasing a bundle of products.

Figure 4-3
MIXED BUNDLING SUMMARY

REASONS TO IMPLEMENT MIXED BUNDLING

- Sell products to customers with different valuations.

- Target price-sensitive customers.

- Remain competitive with rival sellers.

- Use a discount to gain consumer attention.

Next-Best Alternatives

"I'm not willing to pay as much because I have several options to purchase similar products." or *"I'll pay more since I don't have as many options."*

Chapter 1 discussed the role of next-best alternatives in a product's value. Product margins are generally lower in markets with many substitutes compared to those in less competitive areas. The role of next-best alternatives in determining value is why consumers are willing to pay a premium for refreshments from a hotel minibar.

Many retailers incorporate the level of competition (the number of next-best alternatives available to shoppers) in their price-setting process.

- *Giant Food Stores.* The East Coast supermarket chain makes clear: "Prices can vary on specific items in one Giant to another depending on what the grocery store down the road has on sale. We do keep track of what the competition is doing on a regular basis and sort our prices accordingly."[23]
- *Target.* The 1,600-store U.S. retailer admits to charging different prices. "It is commonplace that prices on selected items may vary from Target store to Target store within one metro area," says a company spokesperson. "This is especially true in markets with a high density of Target stores, as well as competitors like Wal-Mart and Kmart."[24] So perhaps Target's motto of "expect more, pay less" should be amended to include "and *even less* in highly competitive areas."
- *Chevron.* The Fortune 25 global energy company also sets prices based on competition. "The fact that there are different prices in different locations is evidence that the competitive marketplace is at work" claims a company spokesperson.[25] The company suggests that a fundamental reason why gas prices in San

Francisco can be significantly higher than those in Los Angeles is because there are fewer gas stations per capita.

The wide availability of next-best alternatives on the Internet, coupled with the ease of purchasing from them, is why prices at websites tend to be lower compared to those at bricks-and-mortar stores. Searching for a better price among physical stores involves considerable effort such as driving to stores, scanning newspapers for sales, and phoning stores.

SELLING TECHNIQUES

The technique used to sell a product can determine a customer's valuation. Differential pricing/selling strategies include holding negotiations, implementing two-part razor/razor-blade pricing, metering usage, and setting prices dynamically.

Negotiation

"This is the price that I'm willing to pay."

Sales forces use negotiation to better understand how much customers value a product. A customer's response to casual questions can reveal his or her willingness to pay. Seemingly innocuous questions have hidden meanings: "What other products are you looking at?" ("What's your next-best alternative?"); "What do you do for a living?" ("How much can you afford?"); "What's your budget?" ("How much are you planning to spend?"). Answers to these questions help skilled negotiators decide how much to charge customers, as well as determine the product attributes that they value highly.

Two-Part Razor/Razor-Blade Pricing

"I use your product frequently and highly value it." or *"I don't use your product very much and am not willing to pay as much as others."*

Two-part razor/razor-blade pricing can be appropriate for products that require an initial purchase of a base product (the razor) as well as additional variable product purchases (the razor blades) that correlate with how much a customer uses (and hence values) a product. This differential pricing tactic is used for products including laser printers and toner cartridges, and video game consoles and game cartridges.

Often the goal of two-part pricing is to use a low razor price to get a product adopted by as many users as possible. For this reason, the razor price is generally set at break-even or a loss. Research company iSuppli estimates that it costs Sony $806 to manufacture a PlayStation 3 video game console with a 20GB hard drive. At its initial suggested retail price of $499, Sony was losing at least $300 on each console.[26]

The payoff comes from purchases of the variable razor-blade product. Printer refill cartridges are brimming with profits. Costing the equivalent of up to $8,000 a gallon, the ink in these refills is one of the most expensive liquids on the planet.[27] It is estimated that 70% of Hewlett-Packard's operating profits are from its imaging and printing division, most of which comes from printer supplies such as toner refills.[28]

A cynic's view of this strategy is that manufacturers set their base price low and then "get you" on the variable product. My view is more charitable: this strategy allows more consumers to benefit from a product. A higher base price would limit the number of customers who could use the product. However, a low base price allows both low-volume users (a home user who purchases one cartridge a year for occasional printing) and higher-volume users (a small business that purchases one cartridge per month) to benefit from the latest printer technology. The ultimate amount of profit derived from a customer depends on usage of the razor-blade product.

Companies can't *require* customers to use their second product. That is against antitrust law. A base product manufacturer can *recommend* its second-part variable product but cannot mandate its use. Other manufacturers often enter the high-profit razor-blade market. Lyra Research estimates that 31.7% of monochrome (black-and-white) laser toner cartridges are sold on the aftermarket (made by non-OEM manufacturers).[29]

This tactic is the opposite of the two-part high/low pricing tactic that I discussed in Chapter 2, which focuses on profiting from the first product price. Why the difference? High/low pricing is best used when the second product *is* competitively priced, while razor/razor-blade pricing is applicable when the second product *isn't* competitively priced.

Consider the incentive created by two-part high/low pricing for members to do the majority of their shopping at Costco. Costco's second product is food and merchandise, which is also sold by many rivals. As a result, Costco chooses to earn its profits from its first part (membership fees) and sell its second parts at low-margin prices. Because of these discounts, customers have an incentive to start their shopping trip at a Costco warehouse, which is often located in lower-cost/less-convenient areas. After making these purchases, members then fill out their shopping needs at local grocery and department stores. This pricing tactic provides Costco with a consistent price advantage in a highly competitive market.

Metering is an alternative to razor/razor blade to appropriately charge low- and high-volume users. Many telecommunication products charge by the number of minutes used. To capture the value of longer-distance moves compared to shorter ones, the moving truck rental agency U-Haul charges $19.95 per day to rent a ten-foot moving truck plus 79 cents per mile.

Dynamic Pricing

So far, every pricing tactic has been framed in terms of satisfying a customer need. Dynamic pricing departs from this convention. This sort
of pricing helps sellers set the right value-based price in unique market
environments through using software that adjusts price according to
demand. Since prices change constantly, this differential pricing tactic
is best suited for products that display prices electronically, such as
via a computer or the Internet (as opposed to on a physical price tag).
Dynamic pricing is applicable to products that are perishable, have
fluctuating demand, or are long-tail (slow-selling but highly profitable
in total).

Perishable products. A type of dynamic pricing, yield management,
is best known for setting prices for fixed-capacity industries that sell
perishable products, such as airlines, hotels, and cruises. The software
monitors consumer demand (for a specific flight, hotel night, or cruise
departure) and changes prices regularly to make the most profit given a
fixed capacity. This is why prices for airline flights, hotels, and cruises
move up and down until the last minute.

Products with fluctuating demand. The value of some products
changes frequently. Demand for a musician's recordings increases
when the musician tours, for instance. Dynamic pricing software de-
tects changes in demand and makes corresponding price adjustments.

Long-tail products. Author Chris Anderson noted the profit potential from selling a large variety of low-volume products. Roughly 25%
of Amazon's book sales come from outside of its top 100,000 titles.[30] It
is almost impossible to manually set prices for a large number of titles
in a manner that captures their value. Dynamic pricing software can
set prices for long-tail products as well as monitor for opportunities to
change prices.

FOCUS ON THE BIG PICTURE:
DISCOUNTS CAN LEAD TO BIGGER PROFITS

Discounts can open the door for customers to purchase a company's most profitable products. This is what David Tuckerman, who as president of distribution for New Line Cinema presided over the global release of the *Lord of the Rings* trilogy of films, learned early in his career.[31]

"Your local cinema isn't in the movie business. It's actually in the soda and popcorn business. That's why they make popcorn in front of you. Back when I was running cinemas, we even tried to vent the smell of fresh popcorn into theaters," David said. "The biggest cost of popcorn and soda was the cups they were served in. But now cups are a profit center because we sell advertising space on them. Oh, and you know those candy machines scattered around the cinema? They are there for you to spend your change on. We want every dime of your change. Theaters make their profit from these ancillary products." Recent statistics support his assertions. The National Association of Theatre Owners claims that as much as 46% of its members' profits come from the concession stand.[32]

David experimented with discount prices when he was the chief operating officer of the Music Makers Theatre chain. Because of increasing interest in watching Monday Night Football, movie attendance dropped from an average of fifty movie-goers for each Monday night showing to just ten patrons. To reverse these losses, David anointed Mondays as Date Night and offered a "buy one, get one free" pricing promotion.

The immediate effects of this discount caused attendance to skyrocket to between 150 and 200 people per showing. Most important, these attendees patronized the concession stand. "While the average Monday customer didn't spend as much as those on a Saturday night did, it was pretty darn close," David relayed with a sense of satisfaction. Since studios got paid a percentage of admissions, they shared the upside of ticket revenue.

With the success of Date Night, Music Maker Theatres expanded the promotion. "Bring your mom, bring your brother, bring whomever, just bring someone," Tuckerman enthusiastically recalled. As a result of this promotion, Mondays became the most profitable off-peak (Monday through Thursday) night for the theater chain.

One surprise from David's pricing experience is that customers didn't "take the discount and run." On Date Nights, thrifty customers drawn in by discounted admission tickets also purchased expensive concessions. I believe that the reason why customers spent their savings is rooted in the mental accounting theory developed by Richard Thaler, a renowned economist.[33] Thaler claims that consumers establish mental accounts for specific occasions. Date Night sales benefited from the effects of this mental accounting. Attendees treated the money saved on admission as an unexpected gain and spent their windfall on concessions that they otherwise would not buy. Additionally, by positioning the discounted night as Date Night, movie-goers viewed this as a different occasion: going on a date. Because of this, additional funds were allocated for their night out.

DIFFERENTIAL PRICING: ORANGE MYPOD PLAYER

Orange can employ differential pricing tactics by offering higher and lower prices.

Lower prices can be offered at warehouse stores, via student discounts, through a $10-off coupon, and to those willing to wait six months after a new model's release. Higher prices can be set at luxury retailers and for customers who want the latest myPod on the day of its release.

DIFFERENTIAL PRICING AND A PRICING WINDFALL

Differential pricing is a strategy that should be used for every product. This pricing practice segments customers with different valuations and sets prices that match their willingness to pay. Higher margins come from tactics such as time in sales cycle and geographic pricing that set higher prices for some customers. Just as important, tactics including coupons and rebates result in lower prices that attract new price-sensitive customers. This results in growth. The profit and growth upside from differential pricing is integral for a company to achieve its financial windfall.

KEY TAKEAWAYS

DIFFERENTIAL PRICING

- Since some customers are willing to pay more than others for a product, companies that set only one price end up in a pricing catch-22. Profits are forgone from customers who would have paid more, while additional customers would have purchased if the price were lower.
- Differential pricing is the strategy of selling the same product at different prices to different customers.
- Differential pricing tactics fall into four categories: (1) hurdles, (2) customer characteristics, (3) selling characteristics, and (4) selling techniques.
- Hurdles involve setting requirements for customers in order to receive a discount, including:

    - Rebates: a reduced price for those who complete paperwork and wait for refund checks.

- Sales: sell periodic discounts to customers unwilling to pay full price.
- Coupons: offer discounts to those who look for, cut out, carry, and redeem coupons.
- Price-match guarantee: match prices of competitors for consumers who prove lower prices.
- Distribution: offer lower prices at less convenient outlets and premium prices at mainstream locations.
- Time in sales cycle: start prices high and then lower over time.

- Customer characteristics provide insights to help identify customers with different valuations. Tactics include:

  - Geography: prices vary by location because of differences in value.
  - Readily identifiable traits: characteristics such as age, status, and proximity to an attraction reveal a different willingness to pay.
  - Club affiliation: in exchange for marketing benefits, discounts are offered to an organization's members.
  - Customer history: a customer's history helps to understand their valuation of a product.

- Selling characteristics can be changed in a manner that allows companies to charge different prices to different customers. These changes include:

  - Quantity: offer a lower per-unit price to those who purchase large quantities.
  - Mixed bundling: create discount bundles that include two or more products.
  - Next-best alternatives: adjust prices in accordance with the

competitive landscape (high-competition markets receive lower prices compared to less competitive areas).

- Selling strategy can be used to determine and capture customer valuations. Tactics include:

  - Negotiation: determines a customer's valuation through discussions.
  - Two part razor/razor-blade pricing: captures different values by making profit from the second product.
  - Metering: captures customer value by metering usage and charging per use.
  - Dynamic pricing: uses software to estimate demand for perishable, fluctuating-value, and long-tail products.

PART THREE

Implementation:
Use Price to Profit and Grow

Up to this point, I've discussed the core ideas, strategies, and tactics involved in creating a comprehensive pricing blossom strategy for products: value-based pricing, pick-a-plan, versioning, and differential pricing. The remaining chapters explain how to use these concepts to create customized pricing blossom strategies that companies can implement to profit and grow. A virtue of the pricing blossom strategy framework is its versatility in solving any pricing challenges that a company may encounter.

Chapter 5 provides step-by-step guidance to create an offensive pricing blossom strategy for products.

Chapter 6 demonstrates how the pricing blossom strategy framework can be used to reset product prices in defensive situations such as recessions, inflation, and entry of a new competitor.

Chapter 7 details how companies can create a culture of profit. This business environment configures a company to implement and fully benefit from better pricing.

5

Offensive Pricing: Create a Pricing Blossom Strategy

PRICING BLOSSOM STRATEGY

Chapters 1 through 4 discussed the core philosophies and initiatives for a company to price for profits and growth. The end result is a comprehensive *pricing blossom strategy*, which is a set of publicly known prices and plans for products composed of:

- A value-based price
- Pricing plans that attract new customers (pick-a-plan)
- Product variations to meet unique customer needs (versioning)
- Higher and lower prices (differential pricing)

The term *pricing blossom* visually describes how to think about and create a comprehensive pricing strategy: the value-based price serves as the foundation from which three strategy "stems" bud out. Each stem

Figure 5-1
PRICING BLOSSOM STRATEGY

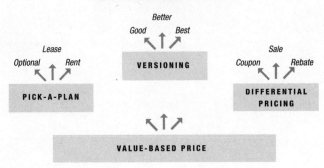

contains several petals that represent the variety of tactics associated with a strategy. Metaphorically, this mix of "strategy stems" and "tactic petals" make a pricing strategy flourish. Creating a pricing blossom strategy will result in every product's pricing windfall.

ORANGE'S PRICING BLOSSOM STRATEGY

The myPod pricing initiatives already discussed result in a set of plans, products, and prices that produce new profits and growth for its manufacturer, Orange. What makes a pricing blossom strategy so powerful is its multifaceted capabilities to capitalize on differing customer values, as well as to offer products and pricing plans that meet the unique needs of various buyers. As a result, this strategy captures the maximum profits for any product.

Think of how much more profit Orange will make by using this pricing blossom strategy compared to its initial "that's the way we always do it" $100 cost-based price. Profits from better margins come from higher prices at Neiman Marcus, customers purchasing on the release date, the premium myPod Touch, and a higher value-based price from

Figure 5-2

FOUR STRATEGIES TO ORANGE'S PRICING WINDFALL

1. SET A VALUE-BASED PRICE	2. ROLLOUT NEW PRICING PLANS	3. OFFER PRODUCT VERSIONS	4. IMPLEMENT DIFFERENTIAL PRICING
Replace the $100 "the way we've always done it" price with $110 value-based price.	Leasing, trade-in option, bundle with unlimited music downloads.	Higher margins: Premium myPod Touch. Lower margins: Stripped-down myPod Shuffle.	Higher prices: Neiman Marcus customers, purchasing on release date. Lower prices: at warehouse stores, student discounts, $10-off coupon, and six months after new release.

the base product. Profits from growth come from new customers drawn to lower prices at warehouse stores, student discounts, the stripped-down version, and discounts offered six months after release, as well as from those attracted to new plans (leasing, trade-in options, and bundles). Given these new income streams, a 1% windfall for Orange seems conservative.

This chapter provides step-by-step guidance to create a pricing blossom strategy for any product. The first part focuses on pricing strategies for B2C companies that sell products directly to retail customers. The next section discusses how to create a pricing blossom strategy for B2B companies that sell to retailers who in turn resell to end users.

SEVEN STEPS TO A B2C PRICING BLOSSOM STRATEGY

The methodology presented in this section is applicable to companies that are setting retail prices for their end-consumers. The following seven steps describe the path that leads companies to their pricing windfall.

Figure 5-3

CREATE A PRICING BLOSSOM STRATEGY

✓ 1. Set a value-based "starting" price.

✓ 2. Offer pick-a-plan strategy alternatives.

✓ 3. Create good, better, and best versions.

✓ 4. Modify product to meet customer needs.

✓ 5. Use differential pricing to provide a range of prices.

✓ 6. Set prices for the tactics in each pricing blossom strategy.

✓ 7. Conduct a cannibalization check.

Step 1: Set a Value-Based "Foundation" Price

A value-based price is the price that the majority of customers purchase a product at and is the foundation of every company's strategy. As discussed in Chapter 1, there are two methods to derive a value-based price. The method to use depends on how many customers are buying a product.

The one-on-one pricing method should be used when selling one unit of a product to one customer (say, a house or one-of-a-kind sports memorabilia). This process involves understanding and setting a price that captures the value that a typical customer places on a product relative to its next-best alternative. After deriving a one-on-one value-based price, do a reality check to ensure that the price at least covers the product's variable costs. To generate profits, this price should be greater than its average total cost.

Most companies face a different challenge: setting a public price to sell many units of a product to more than one customer. Setting prices for professional baseball tickets, for instance. In these circumstances, determining the most profitable price has to take into account that some customers are willing to pay more than others. The first step of this analysis involves creating a demand curve using the multicustomer pricing methodology. The resulting downward-sloping demand curve exhibits the trade-off between price and quantity sold.

After creating a demand curve, the final step is to determine the price (and associated quantity) that garners the highest profit. A high price results in low sales that carry large per-unit margins. Conversely, a lower price yields greater sales but smaller per-unit margins. A profit maximizer analysis involves estimating revenues, costs, and profits at price level intervals and then selecting the price that generates the most profit.

This first step creates a single "foundation" price that captures the value that customers place on a product. The following four steps implement pricing tactics to capitalize on the different prices that customers are willing to pay for a product, as well as to profit by serving the diverse needs of customers interested in purchasing a product.

Figure 5-4 ■ SET A VALUE-BASED "STARTING PRICE"

PRICING METHODOLOGY

	One-on-One	Multicustomer
Selling Situations	One unit of a product to one customer	Many units of a product to more than one customer
Profit Considerations	Ensure that price is greater than variable cost but preferably more than average cost	Conduct a profit maximizer analysis

Step 2: Offer Pick-a-Plan Strategy Alternatives

Pick-a-plan is the strategy designed to satisfy customers' unique pricing plan needs. In addition to, or instead of, selling outright product ownership at one price, implementing a new pricing plan attracts new customers.

Creating new pricing plans involves removing obstacles that block potential customers from making a purchase. New pricing plans tend to have the following characteristics:

New ownership alternatives. Some customers want to use and benefit from a product without owning it. Different ownership plans include interval ownership, lease, rental, and the Netflix model.

Plans that reduce uncertainty in value. Situations when a product's ultimate value is uncertain (concern that the product will not perform or be worth as much as promised) impede purchases. Pricing plans that reduce buyers' risk include success fees, licenses, auctions, and future purchase options.

Price assurance. Many customers prefer a fixed price instead of the uncertainty of a purchase agreement that leaves the final price open-ended ("we'll see how many hours it takes" or "it depends on how much you use"). Plans such as flat rate, peace-of-mind guarantee, all-you-can-eat, and two-part high/low pricing provide the pricing security that customers appreciate.

Plans that help consumers overcome financial and other constraints. Customers may find a price to be acceptable and want to purchase. However, they refrain from buying because of an outside obstacle. Pricing plans that help customers overcome these obstacles include financing, job loss protection, layaway, and prepaid plans.

Figure 5-5
PICK-A-PLAN CHECKLIST

OWNERSHIP ALTERNATIVES	UNCERTAIN VALUE	PRICE ASSURANCE	FINANCIAL & OTHER CONSTRAINTS
❏ Interval ownership	❏ Success fees	❏ Flat rate	❏ Financing
❏ Lease	❏ Licenses	❏ Peace-of-mind	❏ Job loss protection
❏ Rental	❏ Auctions	guarantee	❏ Layaway
❏ Netflix model	❏ Future purchase	❏ All-you-can-eat	❏ Prepaid
	options	❏ Two-part: high/low	
		pricing	

Step 3: Create Good, Better, and Best Versions

Let customers choose from high-priced (more attributes) to low-priced (stripped-down) versions. This type of versioning allows customers to reveal how much they value a product. Those with high valuations purchase the best (margin-packed) version, while customers with a lower willingness to pay opt for the good (modest margin) product. Good, better, and best versions are created by adding or reducing attributes:

Premium (better and best) versions can be constructed with higher quality, guaranteed access, priority access, faster speed, and lower deductibles and improved coverage.

Stripped-down (good) versions are characterized by lower quality, more restrictions, unbundling (à la carte), off-peak times, private-label branding, and higher deductibles and lower benefits.

Figure 5-6
GOOD, BETTER, AND BEST VERSIONING CHECKLIST

PREMIUM	STRIPPED DOWN
❑ Higher quality	❑ Lower quality
❑ Guaranteed access	❑ More restrictions
❑ Priority access	❑ Unbundling (à la carte)
❑ Faster	❑ Off-peak
❑ Low deductibles and better coverage	❑ Private label
	❑ High deductibles and lower benefits

Step 4: Modify Products to Meet Customer Needs

The benefits of versioning are not limited to just profiting from different customer valuations via low- and high-priced options. New customers can be attracted by tweaking product attributes to meet specific needs.

To create need-based versions, consider potential product attributes including package size, warranties, usage purpose, and platforms. Consider offering new selling strategies such as monthly clubs and bundling.

Figure 5-7
VERSIONING TO MEET
CUSTOMER'S NEEDS CHECKLIST

UNIQUE CUSTOMER NEEDS

❑ Package size
❑ Extended and enhanced
   warranties
❑ Usage purpose
❑ Platform
❑ Monthly clubs
❑ Bundling

Step 5: Use Differential Pricing to Provide a Choice of Prices

Differential pricing capitalizes on the unique valuations that customers place on a product by setting a range of low to high prices. This opens the market up to a larger number of customers with varying valuations.

A differential pricing strategy can be employed by:

Creating hurdles. Hurdles require price-sensitive customers to make an effort to receive a discount. Typical hurdles include using rebates, sales, coupons, price match guarantee, distribution outlet, and prices based on time in sales cycle.

Targeting customer characteristics. Prices can be tied to customer characteristics such as geography, readily identifiable traits (being a senior citizen, for instance), club affiliation, and customer history (for example, reckless drivers, previously considered to be uninsurable, can be profitably covered with the right price).

Changing selling characteristics. Prices can differ by changing the selling characteristics of a product (or its environment), such as creating discounts for large quantities, offering mixed bundles, and selling in markets with different next-best alternatives.

Using different selling strategies. Approaches such as negotiation, two-part razor/razor-blade pricing, metering, and dynamic pricing can charge different prices to different customers.

Figure 5-8
DIFFERENTIAL PRICING TACTICS CHECKLIST

HURDLES	CUSTOMER CHARACTERISTICS	PRODUCT CHARACTERISTICS	SELLING STRATEGY
❏ Rebates	❏ Geography	❏ Quantity	❏ Negotiation
❏ Sales	❏ Readily identifiable	❏ Mixed bundles	❏ Two-part:
❏ Coupons	traits	❏ Different next best	razor/razor blade
❏ Price match guarantee	❏ Club affiliation	alternatives	❏ Metering
❏ Distribution	❏ Customer history		❏ Dynamic pricing
❏ Time in sales cycle			

Step 6: Set Prices for Each Pricing Blossom Strategy Tactic

Steps 2 through 5 result in several tactics to help a company price for profits and growth. Now value-based prices need to be set for each of these tactics/options.

Consider the type of analysis that Procter & Gamble had to go through to price the Total Care (best) version of its Tide laundry detergent product. The unique attribute of this premium version is its pledge to keep clothes looking like new over time, even after thirty washes. Since more than one unit is being sold to more than one customer, the following multicustomer pricing methodology should be used.

- Next-best alternative: regular Tide.
- Distinguishing attribute: formulation to keep clothes looking new.
- Use market research, experienced judgment, or past data to create a demand curve.
- Undertake a profit maximizer analysis to determine the most profitable price.

As a result of undertaking such an analysis, a 50-ounce bottle of liquid Tide retails for $9.75, while a 50-ounce package of liquid Tide Total Care sells for $14.99.

The challenge, of course, is in sketching out a demand curve for each product's pricing tactics. This involves using the same three methods described in Chapter 1.

> *Market research*. A market research study can detect how much consumers are willing to pay for an attribute such as a new and improved formulation.
>
> *Past data*. Reviewing the response rates to past coupon campaigns can provide insight as to whether the next coupon should be $1 or $1.50 off in order to achieve more profits.
>
> *Experienced judgment*. A team of product managers can use their combined years of experience to determine the price of the 100-ounce economy-size version.

Step 7: Conduct a Cannibalization Check

This final step involves a critical check to ensure that each tactic in a pricing blossom strategy grows a company's overall profits. The potential downside of employing pick-a-plan, versioning, and differential pricing strategies is that some customers who are currently paying full price will be attracted to the new tactic and end up paying a lower price. This results in profit cannibalization.

The goal of employing pricing tactics is to attract new customers profitably, as well as to continue to earn higher profits from current customers. It's inevitable that some cannibalization will occur, and this is generally acceptable. However, high cannibalization rates can result in lower profits. My experience with firms over the years is that managers become excited about lower-price tactics that can attract new customers. However, many fail to consider the potential losses from cannibalization. Prior to implementing a new pricing tactic, estimates should be made regarding the probability of cannibalization:

High chance. Discounting prices at the beginning of the
season for high-fashion clothes, a time when many
customers are willing to pay a premium for the latest styles,
will most likely result in cannibalized profits.

Medium chance. Starbucks is offering discounted prepaid gift
cards at warehouse stores: $80 buys a $100 credit. While
there are benefits to being marketed at an upscale warehouse club, this promotion is financially beneficial only if it
attracts new customers or spurs current customers to buy
more products than they otherwise would have. The worst
case involves current customers using these prepaid cards
in place of paying full price. If this is the situation, Starbucks receives 70 or so cents on the dollar (after accounting
for the warehouse's markup) instead of full price. The profitability of these discount prepaid cards depends on which
customers buy the cards, as well as if the gift cards are used
in place of regular purchases or to buy additional products.

Low chance. Matching a competitor's price on a comparable
product for a customer who is ready to purchase is generally
win-win. This match generates an incremental sale that
probably otherwise would not have been made. In addition,
this policy can inspire loyalty. Price-sensitive customers
will be attracted to a store because of its "matching
discount" policy.

Most cannibalization checks end up in the "medium chance"
category and therefore require a trade-off analysis. Consider such an
analysis of Hyatt Hotels' policy of offering a 10% discount to AAA
members. Some current customers who are paying full price will now
show their AAA card. This results in a 10% decrease in revenue from
these customers. These margin leaks need to be balanced by growth,
such as new customers attracted to the promotion or current patrons
increasing the frequency of their visits and upgrading their purchases

to more profitable versions (staying in a suite instead of a double room).

By following the seven steps outlined in this section, a comprehensive pricing blossom strategy can be created for any product.

HOW MANY TACTICS SHOULD BE IN A PRICING BLOSSOM STRATEGY?

After working through the above seven steps (especially Steps 2 through 5), it's natural to think, "How many pricing tactics should be offered without confusing customers?" Figure 5-9 provides suggested guidelines to follow when creating a pricing blossom strategy.

Figure 5-9
SUGGESTED PRICING BLOSSOM
STRATEGY GUIDELINES

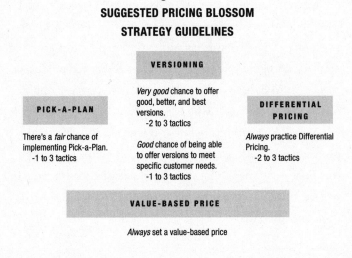

VERSIONING

Very good chance to offer good, better, and best versions.
-2 to 3 tactics

Good chance of being able to offer versions to meet specific customer needs.
-1 to 3 tactics

PICK-A-PLAN

There's a *fair* chance of implementing Pick-a-Plan.
-1 to 3 tactics

DIFFERENTIAL PRICING

Always practice Differential Pricing.
-2 to 3 tactics

VALUE-BASED PRICE

Always set a value-based price

RETAIL PRICING BLOSSOM STRATEGY TEMPLATES

It's straightforward to understand the premise of a pricing blossom framework. However, I have outlined fifty pick-a-plan, versioning, and differential pricing tactics to consider when creating a comprehensible pricing strategy. It's understandable to wonder if some tactics are more relevant than others for a given product.

Since every product faces a unique environment (customer segments, level of competition), it is not possible to specify a set of tactics that fully capitalize on every product's pricing opportunities. However, these templates feature popular pricing tactics for certain types of products. After calculating a value-based price, these templates offer guidance on tactics to include in a pricing blossom strategy.

The following pricing blossom templates are based on the type of product directly sold to consumers:

Professional Services (lawyers, graphic designers, personal trainers)

- Pick-a-plan: financing, success fees, flat rate, all-you-can-eat ("pay a monthly fee and we'll handle everything")
- Versioning: off-peak, employees at different experience levels, retainer (guarantee priority access)
- Differential pricing: quantity, different prices by geography (higher prices in New York compared to Tampa), business type (Fortune 500 versus small business), readily identifiable traits, negotiation, different next-best alternatives

Service Products (restaurants, health clubs, cinemas)

- Pick-a-plan: prepaid, all-you-can-eat
- Versioning: higher and lower qualities, priority access, guaranteed access, off-peak, bundling
- Differential pricing: quantity, coupons, geography, readily identifiable traits, mixed bundles, different next-best alternatives

Retailer (Internet to Main Street to mall stores)

- Pick-a-plan: auctions, future purchase option, two-part high/low pricing, financing, peace-of-mind guarantee, job loss protection, layaway

- Versions: high and low qualities, guaranteed access, priority access, private label, extended and enhanced warranties, monthly clubs
- Differential pricing: rebates, sales, coupons, price match, geography, readily identifiable traits, club affiliation, quantity, mixed bundles, time-in-sales cycle, distribution, negotiation, dynamic pricing

HOW TO CREATE A PRICING
BLOSSOM STRATEGY: MARCO POLO PRICING

The goal of a pricing blossom strategy is to offer a set of tactics that best meets the needs of as many customers as possible and makes each sale at the highest possible price. These are the same hoped-for outcomes of individual negotiations. Car salespeople probe to understand the highest price customers are willing to pay, as well as the pricing plan they desire (sale, lease, financing, high up-front fee plus low monthly payments, low up-front fee plus high monthly payments, and so on). These skilled negotiators ask a series of questions and then, most important, listen for pricing clues. Negotiation is an effective technique to price for profits and growth because it focuses on understanding, serving, and profiting from each customer's needs.

While negotiation is an ideal selling tactic, it's often not feasible for companies to set prices in this manner. Most companies aren't able to evaluate and offer a customized price to each patron. Instead, these companies set prices and plans that are publicly known. A pricing blossom strategy acts as a personal negotiator with each customer (much as a salesperson might). As a skilled sales force does, a pricing blossom strategy recognizes key differences in a customer base and offers a set of prices, products, and plans to profitably serve as many buyers as possible. The beauty of a pricing blossom strategy is that customers self-select into the price and plan that works best for them.

This enables companies to realize the benefits of negotiation without speaking to every customer and avoiding the time (and unpleasantness) often associated with negotiation. This ability to "negotiate" with each customer is why creating a pricing blossom strategy is so important. Just to be clear, offering discount opportunities as part of a pricing blossom strategy doesn't mean that everyone will choose the lowest price. After all, some vacationers will always be willing to pay a premium to vacation during the height of the season.

I use what I call a Marco Polo methodology to create a company's unique pricing blossom strategy. Remember playing Marco Polo when you were a child? In this swimming pool game, the person who is "it" closes his or her eyes while other players (eyes open) spread out around the pool. The goal for the "it" player is to tag another player. To accomplish this, the "it" player yells "Marco" and the other players are required to respond "Polo." Listening for "Polo" clues helps the "it" player tag the closest player. Winning this game requires listening and responding to players.

Creating a comprehensive pricing strategy is much like playing Marco Polo. Companies need to listen for clues from potential customers and respond with the right plans/prices. Here's how the process works:

The seller says: "Marco" ("Here's my product, price, and price plan").

Potential Customers' "Polo"	Seller's Pricing Response
"I need a lower price."	"We run sales. Stay on the lookout."
"I highly value your product."	"Here's our premium version."
"Your ballroom is too expensive for holiday parties."	"We discount holiday parties held in January."
"I won't use it full-time, just occasionally."	"We offer interval ownership."
"I enjoy feeling that I'm getting the lowest prices."	"Become a member for $50 a year and we'll offer you discount prices."
"I'm fine with the price but just don't have all of the money right now."	"We provide an interest-free five-month flex payment plan."

The result of this Marco Polo exercise is a unique pricing blossom strategy, a company's offensive game plan for its product that is based on customer choice. Those who desire the convenience of driving a new car every two years opt for the pick-a-plan tactic of leasing instead of owning. Business travelers who often change their plans pay a premium for a fully refundable hotel reservation version instead of a more restrictive booking. Customers on a tight budget wait to purchase at a company's annual customer appreciation sale (differential pricing) that starts every year at 8:00 A.M. on the third Saturday of February. This customer self-selection process accomplishes exactly what negotiation does: different customers are served with a range of prices and plans.

The takeaway of Marco Polo pricing is simple: listen to customers' needs and address their wishes with a pricing strategy. While market research is a standard technique to learn more about customers, in my experience good information is often available from frontline employees such as sales force and customer representatives. I've moderated many pricing strategy brainstorming sessions at companies and found that the people on the frontlines have an excellent understanding of customers' pricing needs. They interact with and learn from end users as well as wholesale retailers. They watch customers balk at a price that is too high and smile at prices that are lower than what they would have paid, see what attributes customers prefer, and listen to customers discuss what they need from a product and pricing plan. These insights are invaluable in designing a pricing blossom strategy.

To gather and profit from these observations, I suggest that companies host a pricing summit with their frontline. Ask these employees what pick-a-plan, versioning, and differential pricing strategy options customers are seeking. This forum enables companies to channel their employees' experiences and insights into profits. I've found that by the end of these brainstorming sessions, a pricing blossom framework will be filled with suggested pricing tactics that can reap profits and spur growth.

B2B PRICING: SETTING WHOLESALE PRICES FOR RETAILERS

Many companies don't sell their products directly to consumers. Instead, they sell to retailers, who then resell to consumers. Book publishers are B2B companies. They contract with authors, print, and market books. Most publishers sell books to consumers through retailers. This creates a unique situation for B2B companies: retailers feature, sell, and pay for their products. However, end users ultimately determine how many products a B2B company will sell. Because of the impact that both retailers and consumers have on their profits, B2B companies must create a two-stage pricing strategy: one for end users and the other for retailers.

B2B Retail Pricing Blossom

B2B companies have to design a pricing blossom strategy targeted toward the end user who ultimately purchases a product. B2B companies are the primary driver of the pricing plans, versions, and differential pricing tactics that customers encounter. This pricing blossom strategy involves setting a retail value-based price (suggested retail price) as well as creating pick-a-plan, versioning, and differential pricing strategies that serve the widest possible customer base. (See Figure 5-12).

This process for creating a B2B retail pricing blossom is nearly identical to the previously discussed seven steps for a B2C pricing blossom strategy. The only difference is the cost used in the profit maximizer analysis that determines a value-based suggested retail price. As discussed, a profit maximizer analysis determines the retail price (and associated quantity) that earns the most profit. This involves estimating revenue and associated cost at various price points and selecting the price that yields the highest profit for a B2B company. Revenue at each price point comes from the demand curve. The costs used in this analysis should include those incurred for manufacturing as well as the

Figure 5-10
B2B (MANUFACTURER) PROFIT MAXIMIZER ANALYSIS

	RETAIL PRICE PER UNIT	UNITS SOLD	TOTAL REVENUE	MANUFACTURER COSTS	30% RETAIL MARGIN COSTS	TOTAL COSTS	MANUFACTURER PROFITS	
Start at $5 and proceed downwards	$5	20	$100	$20	$30	$50	$50	
	$4	60	$240	$60	$72	$132	$108	
	$3	100	$300	$100	$90	$190	$110	✓ Price that yields the highest B2B profit
	$2	140	$280	$140	$84	$224	$56	
	$1	180	$180	$180	$54	$234	($54)	

Cost = $1 per unit manufactured

Retail Margin = 30% of selling price per unit

Profit Maximizing Suggested Retail Price = $3 (100 units sold)

Resulting wholesale price per product = $2.10 per product [$3 x (1- 30%]).

retail markup. The price that consumers pay is not the amount that a B2B company receives. Instead, it receives this price less the margin that retailers charge. Since retail margin is not realized by B2B companies, it should be counted as a cost to be deducted from customer revenue in a B2B profit maximizer analysis.

The next step involves setting prices and offering options to wholesalers. Setting a wholesale price is commonly achieved through negotiation, as well as "backing it in" from the suggested retail prices. While I don't condone this practice, many stores set retail prices by marking up their wholesale costs or taking a fixed margin from the price that consumers pay. Thus, given a suggested retail price and understanding a retailer's markup policy, a wholesale price can be determined. In Figure 5-10, based on a suggested retail price of $3 and a 30% retail margin, the wholesale price should be $2.10.

Creating and understanding a product's demand curve can also help to better determine the quantity to produce. Producing too many products adversely affects profits. Conversely, manufacturing too few units result in missed opportunities. The TMX Elmo, which keels over in laughter when tickled, sold more than 250,000 units on its first day of sale (a record for the toy industry) and was an immediate sellout.[1]

The remainder of the pricing blossom strategy involves offering wholesale pick-a-plan, versioning, and differential pricing tactics (similar to the ones discussed for end users), which are designed to serve the pricing needs of and profit from contracting with many retailers to sell a product.

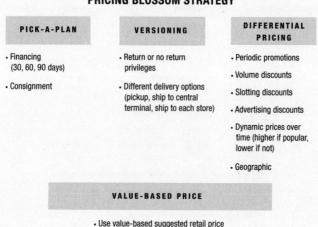

Figure 5-11
BUSINESS-TO-RETAILER
PRICING BLOSSOM STRATEGY

PICK-A-PLAN	VERSIONING	DIFFERENTIAL PRICING
• Financing (30, 60, 90 days)	• Return or no return privileges	• Periodic promotions
• Consignment	• Different delivery options (pickup, ship to central terminal, ship to each store)	• Volume discounts
		• Slotting discounts
		• Advertising discounts
		• Dynamic prices over time (higher if popular, lower if not)
		• Geographic

VALUE-BASED PRICE

• Use value-based suggested retail price to determine wholesale price

It is important to share the rationale and research behind suggested retail prices with stores. While it's a victory to convince retailers to sell a B2B product, the prices that retailers set determine the quantity that consumers will purchase. Thus, retail prices affect the quantity of products that B2B companies sell (hence profits). Given a wholesale price, any price at the suggested retail price *or lower* will generate the highest profits for a retailer. In the publishing industry, the general rule is that publishers charge a wholesale price equal to 50% of the suggested retail price.[2] Once the wholesale price is paid, publishers benefit even more if retailers opt to set prices that are lower than suggested.

Barnes and Noble, for instance, is offering a 40% discount off the list price of Dan Brown's *The Lost Symbol*. Since the wholesale price is the same no matter what retailers charge, publishers benefit when retailers set heavily discounted retail prices.

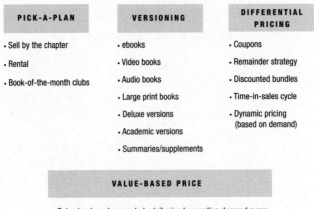

Figure 5-12
B2B RETAIL (BOOK PUBLISHER)
PRICING BLOSSOM STRATEGY

PICK-A-PLAN	VERSIONING	DIFFERENTIAL PRICING
• Sell by the chapter	• ebooks	• Coupons
• Rental	• Video books	• Remainder strategy
• Book-of-the-month clubs	• Audio books	• Discounted bundles
	• Large print books	• Time-in-sales cycle
	• Deluxe versions	• Dynamic pricing (based on demand)
	• Academic versions	
	• Summaries/supplements	

VALUE-BASED PRICE

• Set value-based suggested retail price by creating demand curve and conducting Profit Maximizer analysis

PRICING FOR PROFITS AND GROWTH AT NEW YORK'S METROPOLITAN MUSEUM OF ART

Nonprofits care about pricing just as much as their for-profit counterparts. Since these organizations generally want to serve as many customers as possible, their prices have to encourage growth. However, the urge to set low prices is balanced by the need to produce revenue to improve services. Nonprofit organizations need a pricing strategy that generates profits (to fund improvements) as well as promotes growth (more people benefit from the organization's services). These goals are similar to those of for-profit companies. As a result, the pricing blossom strategy, as well as the concepts and tactics that I have discussed, equally applies to nonprofit organizations.

Consider the pricing challenge faced by New York's Metropolitan Museum of Art. The Met is one of the largest and most comprehensive art museums in the Western hemisphere. The Met's mission statement calls for it to "reach out to the widest possible audience in a spirit of inclusiveness."[3] However, its mission statement also lists the ambition to "enhance the Museum's holdings by acquiring works of art that are the finest and most representative of their kind from around the globe and from all periods of history, including the present."[4] While low admission prices make a museum accessible, the economics of purchasing prized works and commissioning new exhibits require a large budget.

As the senior vice president of external affairs, Harold Holzer oversees the Met's pricing strategy. Harold faces a unique pricing constraint: in exchange for receiving funding from the State of New York, the Met doesn't charge an admission price. However, the Met can *suggest* an admission donation.

Discussing the museum's August 2006 recommended donation increase from $15 to $20, Mr. Holzer focused his explanation on the concept of value. "We moved our price to be in line with the $20 price of the Museum of Modern Art [a next-best alternative], and the Met doesn't charge for special exhibitions like many other museums do [added value]," he reasoned.[5] The museum also employs the differential pricing tactic of charging different prices based on a visitor's characteristics. Lower donations are recommended for seniors ($15), students (free if affiliated with select schools and universities, otherwise $10), and children under 12 (free with an adult). Curious, I had to ask, "Do museum visitors *really* donate?" While Harold couldn't release specific numbers, he did confirm that the average visitor contributes more than $11 per visit.

Using a value-based recommended donation as its foundation price, the Met excels at offering a variety of membership versions. With fifteen annual membership choices ranging from $45 (student) to

$20,000 (President's Circle), the Met had more than 133,000 members in 2008.

What motivates a visitor to pay thousands of dollars for an annual membership when he or she could visit the museum for much less, even for free? The satisfaction of sponsoring a cultural institution is important. But what I found interesting is the value that museum members place on maintaining a *relationship* with the museum. "Members value a relationship with the Met. They want to be in communication with and feel they are a part of the museum," Harold explained. To version this desired attribute, a primary difference between membership tiers is the level of relationship. One of the many benefits of a $12,000 Patron annual membership is an evening program with the museum's director. However, a $20,000 President's Circle membership (there were thirty-five President's Circle members in 2008) includes an evening program with the museum's director as well as a private reception with the museum's president. The Met has done an excellent job of offering different membership levels that provide the value its patrons appreciate.

In addition to memberships that are based on relationship levels, the Met also offers versions to meet members' specific needs. The Met Family Circle is designed for parents and their children ages six to twelve. With programs of interest to both kids and their parents, this membership version promotes the arts to families, develops a constituency for the future, and encourages multigenerational support.

What is interesting about the Met's pricing strategy is how closely it mirrors a for-profit pricing blossom strategy. Starting with a value-based recommended donation, it proceeds to offer good, better, and best membership options, as well as versions to meet specific customer needs. Also, these memberships include an element of pick-a-plan by providing unlimited annual admission.

Up to this point, I've focused on how the Met captures value. But like all organizations, the Met's primary goal is to provide value too. "We have to deliver on the receiving end; we need to exceed our visi-

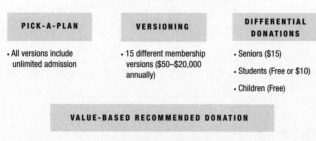

Figure 5-13

THE METROPOLITAN MUSEUM OF ART'S PRICING BLOSSOM STRATEGY

tors' expectations through better performance. Our goal is to continue providing reasons to revisit, because the key to our success is attracting repeat visitors," Harold emphasized. In 2008, for instance, 4.45 million people visited the Met's main building, which was 100,000 more than the previous year.[6] During the same year, the Met also hosted "The Age of Rembrandt: Dutch Paintings in the Metropolitan Museum of Art." This exhibit included all 228 of the museum's Dutch paintings, which is considered to be the greatest collection of Dutch art outside of Europe.[7] Commenting on the strength of this show, Holland Cotter, a *New York Times* art critic, wrote, "The Met has long advertised itself as a grand art multiplex, a cluster of separate world-class museums under a single roof. This isn't just hype; it's true."[8]

From both value and pricing standpoints, the challenges that non-profit organizations face mirror those of for-profit companies.

A PRICING BLOSSOM STRATEGY LEADS TO A FINANCIAL WINDFALL

This chapter brings together all of the book's concepts and tactics to solve the critical challenge that managers at every company in the

world face: "What prices should be set for our products and services?"
A pricing blossom strategy gathers virtually every possible pricing tactic
into an easy-to-follow road map to profits and growth. The resulting
comprehensive pricing strategy collects a company's pricing windfall.

KEY TAKEAWAYS

OFFENSIVE PRICING:
CREATE YOUR PRICING BLOSSOM STRATEGY

- Achieving a 1% windfall involves creating a pricing blossom
  strategy, which is a set of publicly known prices and plans
  for a company's products. It is composed of (1) a value-based
  price, (2) pricing plans that attract new customers (pick-a-plan),
  (3) product variations that meet unique customer needs (versioning), and (4) higher and lower prices (differential pricing).
- Companies face two general types of price setting: retail prices
  (direct to consumers) and wholesale prices (selling to retailers
  that resell to consumers).
- The seven steps to creating a retail pricing blossom strategy
  are:

  1. *Always* set a value-based price.
  2. *Sometimes* offer one or two pick-a-plan tactics to meet
     customers' pricing needs.
  3. *Usually* offer two or three "good, better, best" versions.
  4. *Sometimes* offer one or two product versions to meet
     customers' product needs.
  5. *Always* offer two or three differential prices.
  6. Set prices for each tactic of a pricing blossom strategy.
  7. Conduct a cannibalization check.

- Cannibalization occurs when full paying customers take advantage of new discounts, thus lowering profit margins.
- To help create a customized retail pricing blossom strategy for products sold directly to customers, this chapter offers common pricing tactic templates based on the product sold:

  - Professional services
  - Service product
  - Retailers

- Creating a B2B wholesale pricing blossom strategy involves two phases:

  - Phase 1: create a pricing blossom strategy targeted to end users (those who put a company's products in their shopping baskets).
  - Phase 2: create a pricing blossom strategy to meet the needs of retailers who pay for and stock products.

- Marco Polo pricing is the beginning point for a company to create a pricing blossom strategy. This involves listening to customers' pricing needs and responding with tactics to best serve them.
- Since nonprofits care about profits (to invest in improving services) and growth (more people served), a pricing blossom strategy is important for nonprofit organizations, too.

6

Defensive Pricing: Recession, Inflation, and New Competitors

A COHESIVE PRICING STRATEGY TAMES INFLATION

Unilever, the multinational consumer products company, discovered that a companywide focus on pricing generated new profits in a challenging inflationary market. In early 2007, Unilever's senior management saw its raw material prices start to rise. Concerned about this inflation and the pressure it would place on its profit margins, Bruce Levinson was charged with leading a team to create a best-practice pricing approach.

Bruce, a brand building director in the Unilever Marketing Academy, began by researching how Unilever creates a pricing strategy for the products it sells in over a hundred countries. Working with colleagues on five continents, he investigated how they set and tracked prices for their portfolio of food, home, and personal care products. Bruce was surprised by what he learned, "Our company, which brings in over 40 billion euros in revenues annually, didn't have a uniform global pricing strategy in place," he remarked.[1] Instead, pricing was more of a laissez-faire exercise. "Some parts of Unilever had excellent pricing processes and tools while others had a cursory understanding of pricing," he recalled. "My team assembled together the best of Unilever's pricing capabilities. These best practice concepts helped our managers create and execute pricing strategies that generated new profits to offset mounting raw material price inflation and still maintain consumer value for their favorite brands."

Another issue that Bruce discovered was a lack of consistency regarding which department "owned" the responsibility of setting prices. Sometimes it was Marketing (focused on the role of price in brand positioning); other times it was Finance (which manages the P&L), Customer Development (sales colleagues closest to retail customers and those who make pricing recommendations to the trade), or Consumer & Market Insight (in charge of market data and analysis). He even found a case where each of these departments thought that another was responsible for pricing.

This state of pricing at Unilever is typical. I've found that it's rare for companies of any size to have a coordinated pricing strategy. There are profit opportunities in creating and executing a coordinated company-wide pricing strategy.

Eyeing the benefits of developing a global pricing approach, Bruce set out to clearly define roles and responsibilities and build the pricing skills of the organization. Optimizing prices in each market required coordination of the four departments associated with pricing, as well as clarifying each department's concerns and gaining needed input to the pricing process. After defining each department's responsibilities, Unilever's teams found that the new fully integrated pricing approach "worked like snapping together Lego pieces."

One area that Bruce and his team focused on was identifying price gaps involving powerhouse brands such as Dove, Hellman's, and Lipton. Each of these premium brands has a specific price positioning in the markets in which they are sold around the world. In areas where local price positioning was inconsistent with the global strategy, his team worked with country managers to map out a repricing plan that accounted for the market's unique conditions (consumer types, level of competition, demand).

After creating a best-practices approach, Bruce and his team piloted the program in Europe in 2007. This pilot focused on products facing inflation margin pressure. Assembling the four key pricing departments into one conference room, these pricing workshops sometimes started with a sense of uneasiness. Managing price had never been the most glamorous part of their job, and as a result, the teams had varying levels of confidence. "Pricing was the unloved P of the marketing 4Ps [product, price, promotion, place] at Unilever," Bruce conceded. However, the working sessions were successful by getting everyone into the same pricing mind-set. The group devised tactics based on value and aligned recommended prices with brand strength to combat inflation. In one of the early pilot pricing interventions, these actions led to an 11% increase in operating profits for products at risk from inflation.[2]

This success built buzz within the company, and Unilever rolled out this new pricing practice to its entire global business. And while the immediate effects of these initiatives contributed to price growth of 7.2% in 2008 versus 1.8% in 2007, the highest and longest-lasting return is the confidence that the Unilever organization gained in pricing. "Two years ago, pricing was a low-priority strategy here at Unilever. But today managers recognize its power and the upside potential of getting it right," Bruce relayed with a sense of accomplishment.

As Bruce Levinson learned when he and Unilever faced price inflation, tough economic conditions require companies to focus on their pricing strategy. A well-defined and coordinated strategy can overcome defensive challenges such as inflation, recession, and a new competitor, while continuing to offer consumers the value they seek. Most important, creating a solid pricing foundation for a company will continue to generate profits in the future.

WHEN TO IMPLEMENT DEFENSIVE PRICING

I've focused on using a pricing blossom as an offensive strategy to solve one pricing challenge: "I want to create a pricing strategy to make the most profit from my products." A well-executed pricing blossom strategy enables a company to maximize profits and growth in the current market. However, as I cautioned in Chapter 1, external events can change the value that consumers place on a product.

This chapter provides insights and strategies to respond to three common external changes that affect value:

- *Economic recession.* When consumers' incomes are threatened or reduced, the value they place on products changes. Depending on the product, its value can either rise or fall.
- *Inflation.* Prices for inputs increase, which in turn reduces profit margins.
- *New competitor.* A new rival entering the market often leads to aggressive discounting.

Demonstrating the universal applicability of the pricing blossom strategy to every pricing challenge, the tactics outlined in Chapters 1 through 4 can be used in defensive situations, including recessions and inflation. In these challenging economic environments, demand for products often declines. However, some goods will actually experience an increase in demand. Depending on the type of demand change faced by a product, an increased-demand or decreased-demand pricing blossom strategy should be used. Additionally, a new-competitor pricing blossom strategy can be constructed to handle changes in demand that occur when a new rival enters the market.

PRICING STRATEGY IN A RECESSIONARY ECONOMY

The periodic recessions associated with economic cycles result in a pullback of consumer spending. Higher unemployment reduces disposable income. Just as important, the uncertainty of future income causes some consumers to curtail their purchases. As a result, demand decreases for most products. Interest in premium products wanes as consumers economize, for instance. However, some goods can prosper in a downturn. Sales of private-label products increase as consumers reevaluate the premiums charged for branded products. Whether a product prospers or is challenged in a recession depends how its value fits into the consumer's new buying mind-set.

Demand can drop from consumers shifting into a "trading-down" purchasing mentality in a recession. Trading down is the proclivity to buy cheaper goods and reduce the frequency of purchases. A weeklong annual beach vacation may be replaced by a four-day-long weekend stay or visit to the local amusement park instead.

A trading-down movement primarily occurs for two reasons: income (purchase trade-offs have to be made as personal budgets become constrained or threatened) and taste (when an economy suffers, consumer taste shifts from extravagant to practical; flashy and expensive watches are out while a functional Timex is in).

The 2008 global recession caused the Dow Jones stock market index to drop by 33%, the largest annual drop since the Great Depression.[3] This recession and wealth reduction caused consumers to trade away from higher-priced and nonessential products. Same store sales were down between 8 and 11% at well-known retailers including J. C. Penney, Kohl's, and Target.[4] Additionally, luxury-good sales (defined as the highest priced tenth of jewelry, clothing, and leather products) fell by 34.5%.[5]

In recessions, the products that consumers trade down to (private labels, local amusement park, Timex watches, and so on) benefit from increased demand and the opportunity to reap higher profits. Returning to the 2008 global recession, value-oriented products and discount retailers actually prospered. Same-store sales at McDonald's rose by 8.2% worldwide and net profits were up by 48% for Campbell's Soup.[6] Campbell's profits were boosted in large part due to a price increase that was boldly imposed in the midst of a slumping economy.[7] Even with the price increase, soup as a meal was relatively cost-effective. Similarly, discount retailer Dollar General, which "believes in giving you great values every day," was the biggest 2008 gainer in the S&P 500 Index, with a 36% rise in its stock.[8]

Sainsbury's has also benefited from this consumer trading-down behavior. The British supermarket discovered that instead of going out for meals, its customers were cooking at home and "shopping like a chef" by saving money on staples to splurge on high-end main ingredients (premium fish and meat). Sales of its Basics private-label products surged: rice sales were up 50%, purchases of frozen peas doubled, and pasta sales grew by 300%.[9]

A company's pricing response to a recession depends on whether its product is traded away from or traded down to. Regardless of the situation, companies can create a pricing blossom strategy that will mitigate its downside and possibly generate new profits and growth.

Recession: Products Traded Away From

Most products are traded away from during a recession. The double negative of lower income and a movement toward practicality cuts demand. As a result, the demand curve shifts inward: the number of products sold at each price point decreases.

In stressful economic times, reducing prices is almost a reflexive action for companies. There is comfort in maintaining sales, albeit at lower margins, compared to the uncertainty of maintaining prices and garnering occasional sales at higher margins. While this is understandable, once a price is lowered it is difficult to persuade customers to psychologically reset their product valuation if prices are raised shortly thereafter. A price cut often devalues a product.

It's important to emphasize that a decrease in demand, as brought on by a recession, doesn't mean that *everyone* will stop purchasing at the current price. Instead, fewer consumers will value (hence purchase) a product at a given price. While some will forgo their customary purchases from Godiva in a recession, many will continue to pay full price at the high-end chocolatier. This is important to keep in mind. A decrease in demand is a setback, not an embargo. When facing this situation, companies should implement a decreased-demand pricing blossom strategy. This defensive pricing strategy continues to charge current prices to customers whose valuation is unaffected by the recession. New discount pricing tactics are offered to retain customers who may defect, as well as to attract new price-sensitive customers who previously were not purchasing.

This decreased-demand pricing blossom strategy has several elements:

Pick-a-Plan

Financing and layaway. Help customers with financing plans that meet their financial needs.

All-you-can-eat. This plan satisfies consumers' new focus on value (all-you-can-eat/use for one price) and also provides certainty (the final price is known).

Flat-rate and peace-of-mind guarantee. These pricing offerings also appeal to consumers' increased interest in reducing the uncertainty of the final product price.

Prepaid. A prepaid discount appeals to and locks in purchases from price-sensitive customers.

Auctions. In a recession, consumers become increasingly averse to overpaying for products with an uncertain value. Auctions can quickly establish a product's value.

Success fees. This pricing plan also appeals to risk-averse customers by reducing financial risks.

Figure 6-1
DECREASED DEMAND GENERALLY
LEADS TO LOWER PRICES

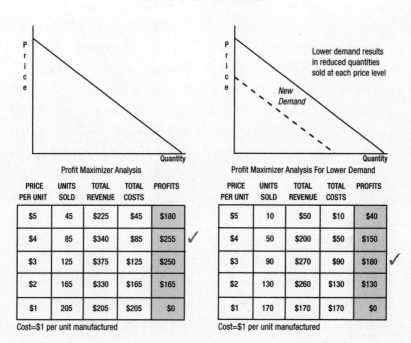

Profit Maximizer Analysis

PRICE PER UNIT	UNITS SOLD	TOTAL REVENUE	TOTAL COSTS	PROFITS	
$5	45	$225	$45	$180	
$4	85	$340	$85	$255	✓
$3	125	$375	$125	$250	
$2	165	$330	$165	$165	
$1	205	$205	$205	$0	

Cost=$1 per unit manufactured

Profit Maximizer Analysis For Lower Demand

PRICE PER UNIT	UNITS SOLD	TOTAL REVENUE	TOTAL COSTS	PROFITS	
$5	10	$50	$10	$40	
$4	50	$200	$50	$150	
$3	90	$270	$90	$180	✓
$2	130	$260	$130	$130	
$1	170	$170	$170	$0	

Cost=$1 per unit manufactured

Two-part high/low pricing. More customers are interested in paying an up-front fee in return for future discounted second-part prices. These plans help to lock in future demand (once the fee is paid, there is an incentive to purchase future second-part products).

Job loss protection. These plans stimulate consumer purchases by offering monthly payment (or order cancellation) insurance in the event of a job loss.

Versioning

Fighter brands. One option is to offer a "fighter brand"—a lower-priced version. If customers are going to defect from a company's flagship products, it is best to sell them discounted versions instead of completely

losing their patronage. Procter & Gamble is known for aggressively versioning its products in tough economic climates. The company offers
cheaper versions of its Pampers diapers and claims that the basic version
of its Bounty paper towels is "priced right up against the private label."[10]

Fighter brands can also be used in situations when consumers are
just not purchasing. This frequently occurs for discretionary products
in economic downturns. With sales dropping by 20% in late 2008,
Chris Martin, CEO of guitar maker C. F. Martin & Co., was in a situation where he "needed something so we wouldn't have to start laying
off people."[11] With its most popular models selling for between $2,000
to $3,000, the company introduced a 1 Series model intended to sell
in the sweet spot of guitar pricing: under $1,000. Resonating with con-
sumers' pricing needs, Martin's first-year 1 Series production of 8,000
guitars sold out promptly.[12]

The benefits of fighter brands are threefold. First, high-valuation
customers continue to pay full price for regular versions. Next, price-sensitive customers purchase the cheaper version. Finally, once the economy
recovers, fighter brands can be withdrawn from the market and their customers transitioned back to paying full price for the flagship product.

Lower-priced products. The general pricing strategy of offering a
tiered good, better, and best product line can be especially profitable in
a down economy. In P&G's case, customers who decide that its signature Tide detergent is too expensive can buy the company's lower-tier
Gain brand. P&G benefits from selling both premium (Pampers) as
well as discounted (Luvs) diapers.

Private label. Both manufacturers and retailers should consider expanding their line of private-label products targeted to price-sensitive
customers.

High deductibles and lower benefits. As a result of consumers econo-
mizing in the downtrodden 2008 economy, many auto insurance customers were dropping collision coverage, increasing their deductibles,
and lowering their coverage limits.[13]

Same price, more product. One avenue to maintain a price point but offer increased value is to include a larger amount or an additional product. Consumer package products can offer "10% more at the same price." The 701 restaurant in Washington, D.C., found success in offering more for a set price. With lunch entrées that range from $15 to $24, the restaurant increased the value it provides with a new three-course lunch menu for $24. On a typical day, 60% of lunch patrons order this value-oriented offering.[14] Service companies can include additional services at the same price. As an incentive to sign up, landscaping companies negotiating summer contracts can throw in extra fertilizing and trimming services for the same price.

Differential Pricing

Sales, coupons, and rebates. These incentives can increase purchase activity. In down times, these tactics make consumers feel virtuous: they make the extra effort and have a visible reward for it.

Negotiation. A slow economy may require a reduction in the "absolute lowest" price that a sales force is authorized to discreetly offer to price-sensitive customers. In addition, if long-standing customers demand a discount (a major buyer asks for a lower price due to the economy), I suggest tying a discount to an event that will reset the current price (such as the stock market rises by 1,500 points).

Geography. Some parts of a region are more severely affected than others in a recession. Because of this, across-the-board pricing actions generally result in granting unnecessary discounts. Companies need to ensure that pricing responses are properly tailored to each region's economic condition.

Quantity. "Value packs" offer discounts to customers who purchase in bulk. Not only does this retain price-sensitive customers, but this tactic also locks up their purchases from competitors (who may desperately discount later). Similarly, volume discounts can be used to mask a discount. Hotels often use "buy three nights and get the fourth free" promotions to maintain a higher room list rate.

Distribution. Follow new consumer buying patterns by selling through outlet and discount stores.

Customer history. Purchasing history reviews can help to identify and target customers who are cutting back due to the recession.

When facing lower demand in a recession, a company's first response should be to maintain the current price and implement a decreased demand pricing blossom strategy. If these actions don't produce satisfactory results, companies should then consider the option of lowering prices. The long-run downside of discounting (in terms of being able to recoup the price cut in the near future) depends on the type of value a product offers: objective or subjective.

The lasting effects of a reduction in a value-based price are less harmful if a product provides objective value (by which I mean the value is more quantifiable—e.g., "using this product saved me from having to perform another task"). In these cases, it's easier to make a price recovery. Suppose a snow removal company lowers its price by 20% (from $50 to $40) during a recession and later tries to return to its initial $50 price. Regardless of the economy, a steep driveway still needs to be cleared of a foot of new snow. Chances are that if a customer was willing to pay $50 before a recession, when the economy improves, the customer will again be willing to pay this price instead of facing the next-best alternative of do-it-yourself shoveling.

The negative repercussions of a discount are more pronounced for products that offer subjective value, which is determined more by personal taste ("this expensive brand is hip"). If premium brands such as Gucci, Montblanc, and Cristal offered 50% discounts during a recession, it would be a challenge to revert to more expensive prices once the economy recovers. Part of a luxury brand's allure is its high price (coupled with the assumption that high price is a signal of quality and exclusivity). Once the economy recovers, consumers will question whether the brand value of a product is really worth the premium.

Figure 6-2
DECREASED DEMAND
PRICING BLOSSOM STRATEGY

PICK-A-PLAN	VERSIONING	DIFFERENTIAL PRICING
• Financing	• Fighter brands	• Sales
• Layaway	• Lower priced products	• Coupons
• All-you-can-eat	• Private label	• Rebates
• Peace of mind guarantee	• Higher deductibles and lower benefits	• Negotiation
• Prepaid	• Same price: more product	• Geography
• Auctions		• Quantity discounts
• Success fees		• Distribution
• Two-part: high/low		• Customer history
• Job loss protection		

VALUE-BASED PRICE
• Maintain current price

Products with highly subjective brand values should avoid drastically lowering prices during a recession.

If it reaches the point that price cuts must be offered, it is best to discuss the issue with customers and couch the issue in terms of the current economic circumstances. Consider a law firm forced to lower prices in a recession. Their discussion with potential clients should be along these lines: "As you know, the poor economy is affecting all business. We have a very talented staff and are trying to minimize layoffs. We currently have excess capacity and are willing to temporarily lower prices to keep our staff busy and ensure that our firm is well positioned for the recovery. Once the economy recovers, we won't be able to offer this discount again. But in the meantime, this is a win-win opportunity to work together and for us to demonstrate the high value of our legal services." This open conversation strikes on understandable compassion (everyone is affected by the economy and appreciates efforts to minimize layoffs), economic realities (utilize excess capacity), solid business sense (be prepared for the upturn), and good opportunity (low price enables clients to try the service). This approach also emphasizes the temporary nature of the discount.

In summary, when facing a trading-away situation:

Step 1. Maintain price and implement a decreased demand pricing blossom strategy.

Step 2. If this defensive pricing blossom strategy doesn't produce satisfactory results, then consider lowering prices as necessary. Remember, it is easier to raise prices in the future for products that offer objective value compared to those providing subjective value.

Recession: Products That Are Traded Down To

Some products thrive in a recession. Products that consumers trade down to will benefit from increased demand. Demand at each price point increases, which provides an opportunity to increase prices—a seemingly contradictory pricing action in a declining economy.

It is risky to raise prices in a down economy. First, it is difficult to know how much further the economy will deteriorate. If the recession deepens, customers may have to make additional trade-away decisions, especially for products that have recently increased their prices. And as the economy regains its strength, those who traded down to a product may return to their normal purchases. This decreased demand will warrant reducing prices. It will be a challenge to communicate lower prices to regain the patronage of a potentially alienated core customer base. Consider price restraint as offering insurance against the effects of a worsening economy, as well as providing the benefit of being positioned to continue profiting once the economy regains strength.

I recommend maintaining (or modestly increasing) prices and

implementing an increased-demand pricing blossom strategy. This strategy aims to keep current customers as well as to provide opportunities to earn higher profits from new customers who are trading down to a product. An increased-demand pricing blossom strategy is made up of:

Pick-a-Plan

Financing. Help customers make purchases in a recession.

Lease and rental. Allow customers to benefit from a product without having to fully own it.

Versions

Higher quality. There is an opportunity to create a higher-quality version targeted to customers who trade down to a product from a more expensive one. To more profitably serve customers trading down in the recent recession, McDonald's rolled out a $4 premium Angus Burger, for instance.[15]

Flat-rate and peace-of-mind guarantee. In a recession, consumers have a greater interest in reducing the uncertainty of the final price of a product.

Differential Pricing

When demand is high, it is possible to reduce differential pricing initiatives. The level of discounts offered, as well as the frequency of rebates, sales, and coupons, can be scaled back.

In summary, for products that are traded down to:

Step 1. Temper price increases.

Step 2. Implement an increased-demand pricing blossom strategy.

Additional profits are earned from more sales and higher margins derived from increased-demand pricing blossom tactics.

Figure 6-3
INCREASED-DEMAND
PRICING BLOSSOM STRATEGY

PICK-A-PLAN	VERSIONING	DIFFERENTIAL PRICING
• Financing	• Higher quality	• Scale down differential pricing tactics including sales, coupons, and rebates
• Leasing	• Flat rate	
• Rental	• Peace-of-mind guarantee	

VALUE-BASED PRICE

• Maintain current price (or temper increases)

PRICING STRATEGY IN AN INFLATIONARY ECONOMY

Another common pricing challenge that companies encounter is a period of price inflation. By this, I mean an economic environment of continually rising raw material and labor costs, which squeezes profit margins. Most managers' impulsive reaction to inflation is to raise prices (pass along higher input costs) to maintain margins. Of course, there is no guarantee that customers will continue to purchase at higher prices.

The best response to inflation is to create a new pricing blossom strategy. The appropriate set of tactics to respond to increased costs depends on the type of inflation: demand-pull or cost-push.

Demand-pull inflation occurs in a strong economy characterized by high consumer demand. This heightened demand causes prices to increase. Companies tend to expand in a strong economy by hiring new workers. With more businesses competing for a limited labor pool, wage rates increase. Businesses pass along these increased costs to consumers via higher prices. Similarly, if high-end resorts experience an increase in demand to hold conferences at their properties, they are inclined to raise prices. In these situations, increased demand from consumers pulls up costs for businesses.

Cost-push inflation occurs when the price of a key input increases. Oil prices peaked at over $147 a barrel in 2008. Since oil is a major component for many products, this shrank profit margins. Airlines were hard hit, as oil went from accounting for roughly 17.5% of their costs to 35% at the peak of oil prices.[16] In a cost-push inflation environment, increased costs cause businesses to push through higher prices.

The adverse effect of price increases associated with cost-push inflation is the economic recession that can occur in this situation. As product prices increase, personal budgets become constrained. This curtails consumer demand. This weakened demand causes company profits to decrease, which results in layoffs and a depressed economy.

Each type of inflation is associated with a different economic environment. Demand-pull occurs in a strong economy, while cost-push usually is associated with a recession. A company's pricing strategy response to inflation depends on whether the economy is booming or entering a slump.

Demand-Pull Inflation

When demand-pull inflation occurs, the value-based price of a product generally increases. This rise is due to:

Demand curve shifting out. In a thriving economy, incomes are increasing and consumer expenditures rise. As a result, more products are purchased at every price level.

Profit maximizer analysis changes. The costs used in profit calculations are now higher, which usually results in a higher price.

Figures 6-1 and 6-4 illustrate the general effects on a value-based price when demand changes, as well as when costs increase. Figure 6-5 summarizes the combination of these demand and cost effects on a value-based price in a 2 × 2 demand/cost matrix.

Figure 6-4

INCREASED COSTS GENERALLY

LEAD TO HIGHER PRICES

Profit Maximizer Analysis
Low Costs

PRICE PER UNIT	UNITS SOLD	TOTAL REVENUE	TOTAL COSTS	PROFITS
$5	10	$50	$10	$40
$4	50	$200	$50	$150
$3	90	$270	$90	$180 ✓
$2	130	$260	$130	$130
$1	170	$170	$170	$0

Cost=$1 per unit manufactured

Profit Maximizer Analysis
High Costs

PRICE PER UNIT	UNITS SOLD	TOTAL REVENUE	TOTAL COSTS	PROFITS
$5	10	$50	$20	$30
$4	50	$200	$100	$100 ✓
$3	90	$270	$180	$90
$2	130	$260	$260	$0
$1	170	$170	$340	($170)

Cost=$2 per unit manufactured

In addition to increasing a product's value-based price, new pricing tactics need to be implemented to capitalize on the increased consumer demand in a prospering economy. This involves implementing a subset of the increased-demand pricing blossom tactics listed in Figure 6-3 (offer higher-quality versions and scale back differential pricing tactics).

If prices need to be raised due to inflation, I suggest having a conversation with (or send a letter to) customers. Point out that input costs have increased, and be specific ("our energy costs have risen by 22%"). I've found that customers appreciate this open dialogue and are more receptive to price increases when they understand the reasons why.

Figure 6-5 ▪ Demand/Cost Effects Matrix

	Demand Decreases	Demand Increases
Costs Same	Decrease price	Increase price
Costs Increase	Ambiguous effect on price	Increase price

Cost-Push Inflation

In cost-push inflation environments, the value-based price for a product changes and new tactics should be implemented. Whether prices increase (or decrease) and which tactics to use depend on how customers treat a product in the accompanying recession: is the product traded down to or traded away from?

If a Product Is Traded Down To

Increase the value-based price. The relevant quadrant of the demand/cost matrix indicates a higher price. Demand increases tend to lead to a price hike. Additionally, for a profit maximizer analysis, cost increases result in higher prices.

Implement an increased-demand pricing blossom strategy. To capitalize on increased demand from customers trading down to a product, the same tactics showcased in the increased-demand pricing blossom can be used (see Figure 6-3).

If a Product Is Traded Away From

Change to value-based price is ambiguous. The relevant quadrant of the demand/cost matrix indicates an ambiguous effect on price. A decrease in demand usually results in a lower price. However, an increase in costs within a profit maximizer analysis leads to a higher price. A more detailed analysis is required to determine the effect on a product's value-based price.

Use a decreased-demand pricing blossom. The pricing tactics used to combat lower demand are virtually the same (except for the "same price, more product" approach) as those highlighted in the decreased-demand pricing blossom (see Figure 6-2).

In this inflationary environment, one additional pricing tactic should be considered:

Same price, less quantity. To avoid increasing prices in a recession, one option is to maintain a price but reduce the amount of product. To keep its prices constant, Breyers ice cream has shrunk its containers from 56 to 48 ounces. The decision to maintain price by decreasing size or increasing price to maintain size depends on the anticipated consumer response.

RESETTING PRICES WHEN A
NEW COMPETITOR ENTERS THE MARKET

While new competition is considered advantageous to consumers (more options, price competition among established players), it's rare for a new entrant to benefit incumbent businesses. A new competitor inevitably steals customers and puts pressure on incumbents to reduce their prices.

For publicly traded companies, the hint of a pricing war from a new entrant can result in a negative reaction from Wall Street. Investors and stock analysts understand that a price war leads to lower profits. The 3M Corporation reported solid quarterly news in October 2007: strong growth and higher 2007 net income expectations. However, the diversified multinational conglomerate, which sells products ranging from dental products to Scotch tape, noted that it would have to discount some of its optical films (used to enhance the brightness and increase the viewing angles of screens such as those on flat-screen television sets) because of competition from low-cost producers. Wall Street reacted swiftly. 3M's shares dropped by 8.6% in one day—that's several billion dollars of market capitalization lost largely because of concerns about the effects of price discounts on 3M's future.[17] Investors might have been more tolerant had the company outlined the defensive pricing tactics it was implementing instead of simply acknowledging that 3M would have to "continue to price down to middle customers."[18]

When a new competitor enters the market, it's natural to consider offering discounts to keep customers from defecting. Resist this temptation. While some customers will sample the competition, many will remain loyal. Why reduce prices to customers who are still willing to pay full price? My advice is to hold steady on prices and create a new-competitor pricing blossom strategy that implements tactics to retain price-sensitive customers as well as attract new buyers.

The first and most critical step is to make sure that everyone in a company, especially those on the frontlines, understands the value of their product relative to the new rival's. This sounds basic, but few companies make the effort to do this. Instead, most go directly into panic discount mode.

It's rare for a new competitor to enter the market with an identical product, as this would virtually guarantee a price war. Instead, new entrants tend to offer a better product (at a higher price) or a product with fewer frills (sold at a discount). It is important to develop a pitch that highlights a product's value relative to the new competition, and feature this pitch in marketing efforts and discussions with customers. This pitch can be along the lines of "True, our rival's product is cheaper, but here are all of the premium attributes that we offer," or "Yes, our competitor does have several additional features, but are these attributes really worth the premium that it is charging?"

Consider an established local electronics retailer negotiating with a customer who has brought in an advertisement from an obscure Internet retailer's site (not a "like" product) and is requesting a price match. Instead of giving in on price and matching the competitor, the value of purchasing from the store should be showcased: (1) the product is available immediately and there are no shipping charges, (2) the local retailer is an authorized service center and all warranty repairs are taken care of on-site, (3) the product can be easily exchanged or refunded at the store if need be, and (4) the store has a long local history and reputation of high service. Once this value is articulated,

Figure 6-6
NEW COMPETITOR
PRICING BLOSSOM STRATEGY

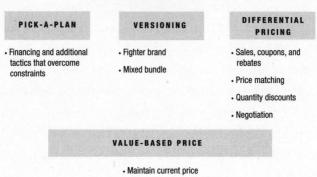

customers will be in a better position to decide if the discounted Internet price is worth the trade-off in benefits from purchasing at a local store.

Once this relative-value pitch is understood by key frontline personnel and incorporated into marketing materials, the next step is to create and implement a new-competition pricing blossom that includes a variety of pricing tactics such as:

Differential Pricing

Sales, coupons, and rebates. Use discounts to retain customers.

Price matching. If the new competitor is offering a lower price (on a "like" product), a matching guarantee can retain customers who would otherwise defect because of price.

Quantity. Offering a quantity discount for a larger size or a contract for a longer time period is a pricing tactic that can lock in customers. In addition to securing larger sales, this blocks sales to the new entrant for the foreseeable future.

Negotiation. If prices are set through negotiation, there's a good chance that buyers will use the new competition to their advantage during pricing discussions. Of course, the first response is to highlight a product's value relative to the competitor. However, if a buyer continues to push for a discount, the next action depends on the outcome of analyzing the possible following scenarios:

Is the buyer bluffing? Every buyer wants a lower price, and a new rival provides an opportunity to push for a discount. Will the buyer really walk away if the price isn't lowered?

Will the buyer accept a compromise of a partial discount? Even better, to maintain the price point in a buyer's mind, instead of offering a discount add new benefits (expedited shipping or financing).

If a discount is granted, will other customers find out? If so, how will this affect price negotiations with other clients?

If a discount is not offered and customers defect, will they come back? Oftentimes B2B customers leave for a rival's discount price only to return because of the incumbent's better value. When a defecting customer returns, consider raising the price. The customer's return states, in essence, "I value your product more than the competitor's."

A discount may make a sale today, but what are the long-run costs? Customers may have been bluffing, may be willing to buy at a compromise discount, or may return after realizing a product's relative value over the new entrant. Additionally, profits will drop if other buyers find out about and start demanding a similar discount.

Versioning

Fighter brand. Instead of involving a signature product in a brand-damaging price war, it is often best to bring in a new product to poach customers from rivals. This is exactly what fast-food chain Burger King did by introducing its discounted Big King sandwich. Advertised as "like a Big Mac, only it has more beef than bread," the Big

King offered 75% more meat and was identical to McDonald's Big Mac in virtually every other respect—yet in promotions it was half the price.

This fighter brand served two purposes. First, in its ongoing price skirmishes with McDonald's, the Big King was the designated "discount product." Price-sensitive customers could purchase this fighter brand. Those less concerned about price would continue paying a premium for the signature Whopper sandwich (which maintained its brand value by not being discounted). Finally, by offering a cheaper and arguably better product than its rival's, the fast-food chain sought to grow by attracting customers. Analysts reported that in its introductory pilots, sales rose as much as 10%.[19] Furthermore, Burger King claimed that in its test marketing, offering the Big King did not cannibalize sales of the company's other burgers.[20] These outcomes demonstrate why, instead of discounting a signature product, introducing a fighter brand may be a better way to defend against and challenge rivals.

Airlines have adopted a similar fighter brand strategy. Previously, when a discount airline entered a market with low prices, incumbents would match or beat its prices on all flights on the contested route. A new entrant's $99 price on its one daily 5:55 P.M. Boston-to-Seattle route would be matched on four of the incumbent's daily flights on this route. Wiser from previous battles, incumbent airlines now create a fighter flight. They maintain prices on their current flights and then add an identical flight, in this case a 5:55 P.M. Boston-to-Seattle flight. In an effort to match the value of the new entrant, discount $99 fares are only available on this fighter flight, not all Boston-to-Seattle flights.

Mixed bundle. Instead of dropping a price, one common tactic is to offer a discounted bundle that includes the key product plus at least one other product (that preferably the competitor doesn't offer). Local appliance sellers can offer a bundle that provides services that a new discount Internet entrant may not be able to match, such as delivery, removal of the old appliance, financing, and service plans.

Pick-a-Plan

Financing and other tactics that overcome constraints. Offering pick-a-plan tactics that activate dormant customers such as financing can provide an advantage over new competitors. Even if entrants match the pricing plan, the overall market size increases because new customers are now able to purchase a product.

In summary, the four steps to combating a new entrant are:

Step 1. Maintaining prices

Step 2. Ensuring that frontline employees understand a product's value relative to the new entrant and that marketing materials highlight this relative value

Step 3. Creating and implementing a new-competitor pricing blossom strategy

Step 4. Being more aggressive with price discounts (as a last resort) if the results of employing a pricing blossom strategy are not satisfactory

RECESSIONS, INFLATION, AND NEW COMPETITORS

A pricing blossom strategy contains a mix of pricing tactics designed to maximize profits and generate growth in every market environment. The universal applicability of the pricing blossom strategy framework is relevant for companies that are facing pricing challenges, including recessions, inflation, and new competitors. These market developments change the value that *some* customers place on a product. This requires companies to amend their pricing strategy. Even in these challenging environments, a pricing blossom strategy can increase profits by retaining current customers as well as adding new ones.

There are some occasions in recessionary and inflationary market environments when demand increases for a product. New profits and growth can be realized in these economic situations by:

1. Capitalizing on new demand by selling to more customers
2. Offering higher-quality (and premium-priced) versions to customers who are trading down to a product
3. Reducing discount opportunities to current customers

There are many situations (new competitor, recession, and inflation) when demand for a product decreases. In these cases, a pricing blossom strategy can be implemented that maintains price and implements a series of discount tactics. Decreased-demand and new-competitor pricing strategy blossoms turn around weak demand by:

1. Selling at full price to current customers who aren't defecting
2. Offering discount pricing tactics to retain customers who may leave due to price
3. Attracting price-sensitive customers from rivals that aren't amending their pricing strategy in these situations
4. Adding new pricing plans that generate growth by making a product accessible to new customers

Figure 6-7

SUMMARY OF RECESSION, INFLATION,
AND NEW-COMPETITOR PRICING STRATEGIES

EXTERNAL CHANGE	INITIAL EFFECT ON VALUE-BASED PRICE	PRICING BLOSSOM STRATEGY
Recession/Traded away from	Maintain	Decreased demand
Recession/Traded down to	Maintain	Increased demand
Demand-pull inflation	Increase	Increased demand (subset of tactics)
Cost-push inflation/ Traded down to	Increase	Increased demand
Cost-push inflation/ Traded away from	Ambiguous	Decreased demand
New competitor	Maintain	New competitor

KEY TAKEAWAYS

DEFENSIVE PRICING: RECESSION, INFLATION, AND NEW COMPETITORS

- Three major market changes that require companies to reset their pricing strategy are recession, inflation, and entry of a new competitor.
- The effects of a recession can lead to a product being traded away from (decreased demand) or traded down to (increased demand).

  - "Traded away from" strategy: maintain price and create a decreased-demand pricing blossom strategy that offers discount opportunities.

- "Traded down to" strategy: maintain price (or temper increases) and create an increased-demand pricing blossom strategy that increases margins.

- Inflation can be classified as:

  - Demand-pull: a strong economy can cause the prices of inputs to rise, which reduces profit margins.
  - Cost-push: a change in a key input price (oil, for example) causes upward price pressure. The resulting price increases can push an economy into a recession.

- Demand-pull inflation strategy: raise value-based price and implement a subset of tactics in an increased-demand pricing blossom strategy (offer higher-quality versions and scale back differential pricing tactics).
- The pricing response to cost-push inflation depends on whether a product is traded down to or traded away from.

  - "Traded down to" strategy: raise value-based price and use an increased-demand pricing blossom strategy.
  - "Traded away from" strategy: it's ambiguous whether to increase or decrease a value-based price. Create a decreased-demand pricing blossom strategy.

- A new rival entering the market often results in pricing pressure. The pricing response to a new competitor involves maintaining the current value-based price, establishing and communicating relative value, and creating a new-competitor pricing blossom strategy that provides discount opportunities, locks in customer demand, and attracts new customers.

7

Create a Culture of Profit

**A COMPANY ENVIRONMENT THAT
PROMOTES PROFITS AND GROWTH**

Up to this point, I've discussed ideas and tactics to set prices in offensive and defensive situations. This knowledge is critical. However, creating and implementing a pricing blossom strategy requires many people in a company to buy in to the pricing philosophies and to be proactive in their efforts. After all, it takes a team of employees to successfully design and execute a pricing blossom strategy. Consider a NASCAR driver who wants to win a race. The skill of being an excellent driver is necessary. Yet having the right equipment and team is equally crucial to crossing the finish line ahead of competitors. This is also true of pricing. For a company to price for profits and growth, the right skills, teamwork, and processes need to be in place. This chapter discusses the philosophies, foundations, and ongoing initiatives necessary for a company to excel in and benefit from better pricing.

A culture of profit is a business environment that supports and encourages employees of a company to price for profits and growth. The first step to creating this culture involves reaching consensus about the objectives and actions necessary to succeed. This agreement is necessary for a team to work together cohesively. As I've mentioned, managers often hold divergent pricing philosophies. This results in the perpetuation of several pricing myths (and associated practices) within a company that must be corrected. Next, confidence must be instilled within a company to understand and capture the value of its products. Finally, tools and information need to be provided to help employees implement better pricing practices.

The principles of a culture of profit support a company in its quest to reap a pricing windfall. Building these profit pillars into an organization's ethos creates a pricing foundation that will stand the test of time, market conditions, and new employees. While these principles may appear to be elementary, there is a significant upside for companies to ensure that these fundamentals are in place. Illustrating the benefits of focusing on the essentials, a study published in the *New England Journal of Medicine* researched the effects of undertaking a nineteen-point "basics" surgical safety checklist in medical operating rooms. This common sense list includes steps such as:

- Ask the person's name to make sure the right patient is being operated on.
- Confirm that blood supply is available if blood loss is expected.
- Account for all sponges, needles, and instruments after surgery to ensure that nothing is left in the patient.

The benefits of mandating the use of this checklist were impressive: the death rate was cut by almost half and complications reduced by a third. Additionally, the study estimated that if these fundamentals are implemented in all U.S. operating rooms, at least $15 billion will be saved annually.[1] Elaborating on the value of having everyone involved with a surgery follow these basic procedures, one of the study's authors commented, "What we are seeing are the benefits of good teamwork and coordinated care."[2] This is exactly what a culture of profit accomplishes for a company: good teamwork and coordinated actions lead to increased profits and growth.

Figure 7-1
CULTURE OF PROFIT PRINCIPLES

PHILOSOPHIES: BREAK THE MYTHS	FOUNDATIONS: CREATE CONFIDENCE IN THE PRODUCT	ONGOING INITIATIVES: BEST PRACTICES FOR PROFIT
• Set prices to capture value. • It is possible to achieve the largest market share *and* highest profits. • High volume customers don't have to receive the lowest prices. • A discount today doesn't guarantee a premium tomorrow. • Higher operating profit margins are not a sign of better pricing.	• Create a value statement. • Reinforce that it is okay to earn profits.	• Speak and sell in terms of net prices. • Organize and collect competitive information. • Monitor the value of products. • Incorporate profitability into compensation packages. • Host peridoic pricing roundtables.

The principles that make up a culture of profit are categorized into three general groups: philosophies, foundations, and ongoing initiatives.

PHILOSOPHIES—BREAK THE MYTHS

It is important that key members of a company—from executives on the top floor at headquarters to those on the sales floor on Main Street—be in agreement on the fundamental principles of setting prices. Staff members often hold "the earth is flat" ideas about pricing that need to be changed before a company can reap its financial windfall. The six most common myths that need to be broken are:

- Myth 1: Setting prices involves marking up prices (cost-plus).
- Myth 2: Increasing market share involves a trade-off between price and share.
- Myth 3: The highest-volume customers should receive the lowest prices.
- Myth 4: Discounting to get in the door will lead to premiums once a product proves its value to customers.
- Myth 5: Higher operating margins signify pricing excellence.
- Myth 6: Lower prices to regain lost volume.

Principle 1: Set Prices to Capture the Value Customers Place on a Product

Marking up costs by a certain percentage or using "the way that we always have done it" methods often have become part of a company's culture. Since a value-based price should be the foundation of every company's pricing strategy, this "capture the product's value" mind-set must be communicated to and adopted by staff members.

To change the pricing mind-set within a company, I suggest a three-step process of anecdotes, personal experiences, and fact-based case studies. I've found that people appreciate and understand the umbrella pricing strategy that I wrote about in the Introduction. This simple story provides the intuition behind capturing value: Manhattan street vendors raise umbrella prices when it looks as if it will (or starts to) rain. This price increase has nothing to do with a change in cost; instead it's all about the increased value that customers place on rain protection. Next, emphasize that since consumers are the ones who make purchases, their buying process has to be understood. Ask staff members how they evaluate prices for their personal purchases. Do they estimate the cost of a product and have a strict rule of purchasing only if this cost is marked up by 50% (or less)? Most don't. Instead, consumers evaluate a product by comparing it with its next-best alternatives and selecting the one that offers the best value (in terms of both price and attributes). In other words, they make pricing decisions based on the value provided by a product. Finally, discuss a few pertinent stories such as the Parker Hannifin (industrial products), Lafarge (fly ash), and SmugMug (digital picture sharing) examples featured earlier. These case studies showcase the new profits earned by companies that focused their pricing strategy on capturing value.

The above process provides the intuition of value-based pricing, reveals that the consumer buying process is identical to how staff members evaluate their own personal purchases, and provides inspirational examples of managers who have reaped pricing windfalls by successfully implementing value-based prices. This reasoning is compelling and can convince employees that value-based pricing is the best approach to setting prices.

Principle 2: It Is Possible to Achieve Both the Largest Market Share and Highest Profits

Conventional business wisdom assumes that prices must be heavily discounted for a company to become a market share leader. In other words, this adage claims that there is a trade-off between price and market share. This thinking comes directly from the inverse relationship between price and quantity in a demand curve: a higher price leads to lower quantity sold and vice versa. As a result, companies seeking a higher market share believe that the only way of doing so is through setting bargain prices. But gaining market share in this manner rarely results in the highest profit for a company.

The presumed trade-off between price and market share is based on the assumption that companies offer only one price (akin to the idea that only one optimal price can be selected on a demand curve). However, recall that a pricing blossom strategy offers a variety of prices and plans for a product. Consider the margin and growth opportunities of pursuing market share by implementing a pricing blossom strategy instead of only using one bargain price:

- The value-based list price in a pricing blossom strategy will be higher.
- Pick-a-plan tactics generate growth by selling to new customers who otherwise would not purchase.
- Premium differential pricing tactics, as well as "best" versions, produce higher margins. Additionally, some new customers come specifically for the best version.
- Discounted differential pricing tactics and lower-priced "good" versions attract more customers. Additionally, the higher prices paid by some can subsidize prices for others. Early-bird prices (that cover variable costs and contribute to overhead) can be even lower than the single bargain price offered by a rival, for instance. These discount tactics enable a company to serve more customers.

By targeting customer segments through pick-a-plan, versioning, and differential pricing tactics, the maximum number of customers can be serviced. Additionally, by offering high- and low-price choices, consumers reveal (and are charged) the value that they place on a product. This produces the highest possible profits.

Consider the profit and growth benefits for a chef seeking higher market share by implementing a pricing blossom strategy instead of just setting bargain prices. Premium-priced chef's table and private dining versions provide higher profits. Discount pricing tactics (such as coupons, early-bird specials, "buy five get one free" punch cards, senior citizen discounts, off-peak Tuesday specials, and so on) generate growth.

Principle 3: High-Volume Customers
Don't Have to Receive the Lowest Prices

Many managers believe that their biggest clients are entitled to receive the best prices. Of course, it is important to express gratitude to high-volume buyers. However, offering unnecessary discounts isn't always warranted (why give away money unless the customer asks?), nor is this practice profitable for a company. Additionally, discounts are often gifts that unintentionally continue to give: they become grandfathered into future contracts and customers expect lower prices in the future. There are several other methods to show appreciation to top accounts. Reserve discounts to attract price-sensitive buyers who need an extra incentive to purchase.

Principle 4: A Discount Today Doesn't Guarantee a Premium Tomorrow

It's common for sales managers to offer a discount based on the hope that after a customer tries and realizes the value of a product, the consumer will accept a price increase. This reasoning is understandable. I regularly meet salespeople who believe in this practice, but less frequently do I find ones who have successfully passed through a price increase. Especially for expensive products that offer subjective value (a premium brand, for instance), a discount usually diminishes the value that customers place on a product. As a result, once a product's price is lowered, it is a challenge to convince customers to pay more in the future.

There is more leeway in this principle for lower-priced products that offer less subjective value. Coupons, such as those in Sunday newspaper inserts, provide three benefits for companies. First, there is marketing value in having a one-page insert that showcases the value-based attributes of a product. Next, coupons serve the price-sensitive who wait to purchase at a discount. Finally, coupons inspire trial, which may later lead to full-price purchases.

There are other low-risk avenues to prove a product's value. Satisfaction-guaranteed or money-back offers are a bold backing of pledged value. A trial size or service (a small project, for instance) can also encourage customers to evaluate a product. Finally, if neither of these options is viable, consider offering a trial rebate. For a product (or service used during a set period), customers pay full price and at a later date receive a rebate discount check. The goal of this technique is to provide an incentive for trial while establishing the full price in customers' minds.

Principle 5: Higher Operating Margins Are Not a Sign of Better Pricing

Many executives view increased operating margins as a metric of success for pricing initiatives. Holding costs constant, a higher operating margin often signifies that the average price has increased. From my perspective, higher margins can indicate that opportunities to sell to price-sensitive customers are being missed. When discount tactics to serve these customers are implemented, additional profits are earned. However, since prices are lower, the overall operating margin may decline. The best metric to evaluate the success of a pricing initiative is straightforward: is the company earning more profit than it was before?

Principle 6: An Across-the-Board Discount Is Not the Best Response to the Problem of Reduced Sales Volume

It is painful when sales volume drops significantly—say, by 15%. This lower volume can swing a company from a profit to a loss. It's instinctive for managers to focus on this lost 15% and slash prices to regain volume. However, I prefer to view this situation differently: customers who are responsible for 85% of the volume sold are continuing to pay full price. Instead of lowering prices across the board, targeted decreased-demand pricing blossom strategy discount tactics as discussed in Chapter 6 should be offered to regain lost volume and attract new price-sensitive customers.

FOUNDATIONS: CREATE CONFIDENCE IN THE PRODUCT

To improve sales as well as increase staff morale, it is essential to instill confidence in employees about the value of the products that they sell. This involves creating a value statement to ensure that employees are comfortable with setting prices that capture consumer value.

Principle 7: Create a Value Statement

My first question to managers who are interested in improving their pricing strategies is, "How does your product differ from those sold by competitors?" After a few minutes of consideration, the typical response is a nondescriptive "ours is better." This is disappointing. Providing value is the cornerstone of a company's existence—if a product doesn't offer consumers a unique value, there is no reason for them to purchase. A product's unique value is what leads customers to the checkout counter. If staff members don't understand the value of the products they sell, neither will potential customers.

It's critical for companies to create a value statement for their products. By a value statement, I mean a communication that articulates the value of a product relative to its next-best alternatives. The essence of this declaration amounts to "here's why we are so proud of our product and why customers should buy it over the competition." Be more specific than "ours is better" because this is not an occasion to be modest. List every major positive attribute: "*Consumer Reports* rated ours the best," "Nine out of ten people surveyed prefer our product in a blind taste test," "We have a 98% delivery fill rate," "Our product is eco-friendly," and so on. Since the attributes that make up a product's value are multifaceted, staff members throughout a company (product design, marketing, distribution, and sales force, for example) should participate in putting together this proclamation. Each department should be encouraged to brag about the unique product value they provide to customers.

After creating a value statement, the next step is to discuss it with *everyone* in a company. I recommend that everyone understand this value statement for two reasons. First, it is critical for a company's frontline personnel to buy in to this value statement—this summary sheet supports their daily efforts to educate customers about, promote, and sell products. Just as important, a value statement boosts morale within a company. I've worked with many companies whose products seem mundane at first glance. But what makes a product interesting, even one that initially appears drab, is the unique value that it offers to consumers. After all, where would we be without paper clips and lightbulbs?

When I moderate sessions to determine a product's value, audiences perk up when I solicit ideas on what makes their product stand out from rivals. Employees are interested in learning what makes their company's products distinctive. They want to be proud of the products that they sell. I see their pride when I mention that customers who make purchases have investigated the market, "test-driven" rivals' products, and concluded that their product offers something special that no other competitor provides. A value statement allows employees to fully comprehend the good that their products offer consumers. Showcasing the value of their products helps to validate their job and makes them feel proud of the work that they do.

After creating and conveying a value statement, everyone in a company should be able to confidently segue into a two-minute "here's why we are so great" pitch when asked by a potential customer (or stranger at a party), "Tell me about your company and its product."

Principle 8: Reinforce That It Is Okay to Earn Profits

This topic should be discussed in tandem with the value statement presentation. I've found that even normally gregarious people become shy when discussing their product's price. This uneasiness comes from a lack of confidence in their products, as well as the role of price in the personal relationships that often develops with customers.

It's uncomfortable for a salesperson to propose a price if he or she can't rationalize it to him- or herself. This is why a value statement is important: it provides frontline employees with the confidence to offer and justify a price to potential customers. Additionally, I've found that employees appreciate being reminded that when a purchase is made, customers are in essence saying, "Thank you—your product offers me the best value relative to the alternatives." This reinforces that customers find the product and its price to be a good deal. Finally, it is helpful to reiterate that a company's pricing blossom strategy is based on offering customers choices. Customers select the price, version, or pricing plan that works best for them.

When frontline staff work with customers, the interaction often takes on a personal tone. This relationship can range from a brief chat to long-term friendships. Personal relationships can cloud the goal of fully capturing customer value: "Should I charge my friend the full price?" One way for a salesperson to be nice is to offer an unexpected (and unnecessary) discount. And while this can make customers happy, this generosity comes at the expense of the company's operating profits. It's critical to emphasize that companies are in business to make profits and are entitled to do so. I've found that once the frontline people understand the upside effects of a 1% price increase, they become conservative in volunteering discounts. It's also important to note that customers who have become friends may consequently defect for a rival's lower price. After all, it is often the job of consumers and corporate buyers to purchase comparable products at the best price. A friendship predicated on offering discounts has no loyalty.

The ultimate goal of creating a value statement, instilling confidence, and explaining the reasons for setting prices to capture value is for the frontline people to be able to have a comfortable pricing discussion with customers. This preparation builds their ability to look customers steadily in the eye and convincingly showcase a product's value, justify its price, and emphasize what a great value their product offers. This confidence and focus on profit are especially critical as companies cede more control of prices to employees. Many retailers, including Home Depot, now allow their employees to negotiate with customers to make a sale. Commenting on this new practice, a Home Depot spokesperson claims, "We want to work with the customer, and if that happens to mean negotiating a price, then we're willing to look at that."[3]

ONGOING INITIATIVES—BEST PRACTICES FOR PROFIT

At this point in creating a culture of profit, agreement has been reached on pricing philosophies and employees understand the value of a product and the goal of setting prices to capture value. The final step is to undertake initiatives that provide information, incentives, and support to help staff members succeed in better pricing. These initiatives include focusing on net prices, tracking competitors, monitoring changes in a product's value, providing financial incentives for the frontline personnel to push for higher prices, and soliciting intelligence (on consumers as well as competitors) and best practices from employees.

Principle 9: Speak and Sell in Terms of Net Prices

All B2B companies should undertake a "waterfall analysis."[4] It is rare for the invoice price listed on a purchase order to be the actual amount that a company collects. A variety of off-invoice discounts are commonly offered in B2B transactions, including annual volume rebates, financing options (cash, 30-, 60-, or 90-day payment deadlines), freight options (deliver to central warehouse, deliver to individual stores, or the client picks up), and various other payments (advertising, slotting, stocking).[5] B2B manufacturers often utilize as many as fifty different types of off-invoice discounts in their sales practices. These discounts can add up on an order and significantly reduce the ultimate amount received by companies.

A waterfall analysis examines each account and strips off every discount attached to an invoice price. This discount delayering process determines how much money a company is really earning from each invoice price. This analysis usually results in the following:

- *Shock.* Every analysis I've conducted yields surprises. Invoice prices that appear attractive end up disappointing after all discounts are stripped off. Conversely, many seemingly low margin prices look better when fairly compared to other net invoice prices. This information often changes priorities: some accounts start to receive better treatment, while others are singled out for margin improvement negotiations.
- *Enforcement.* A waterfall analysis inevitably reveals that some buyers are receiving volume-based discounts (a 15% discount based on a pledge of $500,000 in orders annually, for instance) but aren't meeting their obligations. These buyers should be reminded of their promise and offered the option to forgo their discount if they cannot meet their pledge.
- *Revaluation.* B2B discounts attached to a renewable contract often accumulate over time. A discount that made sense to offer ten years ago may remain unnecessarily in place today. A waterfall analysis allows companies to reexamine the discounts that each account receives and adjust prices accordingly. The usual conclusion of this analysis is to take a "not valid with any other offers or discounts" stance toward customers who have additively benefited from discounts accrued over time.
- *Convergence.* A lesson learned from every waterfall analysis is that invoice prices are deceiving. Prices should be listed and spoken of in terms of net prices, the amount that a purchaser actually pays for an order.

Offering an array of discounts is often ingrained in the manner that companies do business. Often times it is simply "known" within a company that certain retailers always are granted discounts such as a 15% quarterly rebate. It is difficult to wean a sales force from offering discounts that have been long considered a regular part of doing business.

Of course, if these discounts are necessary to remain competitive, they should remain in place. However, in most cases these profit drains remain in place due to inertia as well as to avoid potential pushback from longtime buyers who have become accustomed to receiving preferential prices.

Principle 10: Organize and Collect Competitive Information

Recall that a product's value depends on how it compares (in terms of availability, attributes, and price) to its next-best alternatives. To set prices for a product, the key characteristics and prices of competing products have to be known. Better understanding the competition is essential to creating a value statement, developing a sales pitch, and setting a price.

Since competing products play a critical role in defining a product's value, companies need to create a competitive intelligence system (or at least a mind-set). This system should organize information on rivals' products, prices, past promotions, current clients, and general pricing behavior (history of maintaining prices or aggressively discounting to make the sale), as well as rumors of their actions. Employees need to be proactively encouraged to collect and report competitor information. When it's time to readjust prices or bid on a contract, these data are valuable.

Principle 11: Monitor the Value of Products

Deriving a value-based price is an essential start, but real success is the ability to adjust a product's price as its value changes. The process of losing weight is an appropriate analogy that illustrates the importance of continuity: while it's a coup to lose twenty pounds, true success is maintaining this loss over time.

To keep prices consistent with value, companies need to build a value-and-cost-monitoring system, or at least institute periodic "right price" evaluations that check if:

- The economy (thus consumer budgets) is shifting.
- New competition is on the horizon.
- Prices of close and extended substitutes are changing.
- Consumers are behaving differently due to evolving tastes.
- Competitors are offering new products.
- Prices of complementary goods are changing.
- Key input prices are fluctuating (which requires a new profit maximizer analysis).

It was Unilever's early detection of changing input prices that focused the company on better pricing. The resulting initiatives enabled Unilever to thrive in both recessionary and inflationary market environments.

Principle 12: Incorporate Profitability into Compensation Packages

Many companies pay their sales force a commission that is based on the dollar volume sold, not on the profitability of sales. This compensation system offers salespeople little motivation to price in a manner that is most beneficial to their employers. To understand the low interest in profits that is created by paying commissions based on volume, consider the decisions faced by the sales force. If a salesperson is paid based on the dollar amount of volume sold (say, 5%), the incremental amount earned by increasing a "sure to order" $100,000 price tag to a more profitable $105,000 is minimal. However, the risk of alienating a client with the higher price increases significantly. Since there is such a small upside to the salesperson's paycheck from taking this risk, there is little incentive to push for higher prices.

Incorporating profitability into the sales force's commission structure provides a reason for a salesperson to spend an extra thirty minutes with a client to highlight the product's value. This incentive to capture value ensures that these employees, who control a key lever of a company's bottom line (revenue), focus on profits. In the above example, if the sale becomes profitable only if it's over $90,000, the commission structure could be 35% of revenue over this profit-loss threshold. By basing compensation on profits, the sales force wins only when the company wins.

Instituting a new compensation system that rewards higher margins requires providing sensitive profit information to the sales force. Many salespeople don't know the profit margins on the products that they sell or accounts they service. The downside of sharing this data is that if an employee moves to a competitor, this confidential information may be compromised. However, without this information or guidance, a sales force is left in the dark and unable to sell in a manner that best benefits their company.

Figure 7-2 ■ Compensation Based on Profit Provides Incentives for a Sales Force to Focus on the Bottom Line

---

Consider the economics of a $100,000 sale with a 5% volume commission:

- Sales commission: $100,000 × 5% = $5,000

- Company profit: $100,000 – $5,000 (commission) – $90,000 (cost) = $5,000

Alternatively, consider a commission equal to 35% of profits. Suppose this new compensation structure encourages a salesperson to work harder for a higher price of $105,000. Both the salesperson and the company benefit from this extra effort:

- Sales commission: $105,000 – $90,000 (cost) = $15,000

- The salesperson earns $5,250 ($15,000 × 35%)

- Company profit: $105,000 – $5,250 (commission) – $90,000 (cost) = $9,750

Principle 13: Host Periodic Pricing Roundtables

Since many people in a company are affected by and touch price, there is genuine interest in the topic. Additionally, it is important to keep up on pricing issues because variables that affect price constantly change. For these two reasons, I suggest hosting regular roundtables to discuss pricing.

When I work on-site with companies on their pricing strategy, I am often offered an office in the sales and marketing area. Throughout the day, I overhear executives discussing prices with each other as well as with clients. In these daily discussions, employees accumulate considerable knowledge that can help others in their company overcome pricing challenges when this information is shared.

I've found that frontline employees enjoy discussing their pricing challenges and experiences—pricing is a big part of their workday. Roundtable events provide staff members the opportunity to share tips, trends, and success stories, as well as constructively criticize their company's pricing process. To reinforce the high priority of pricing, senior management should participate in and provide encouragement at these meetings.

A structured pricing discussion provides actionable insights. It is important to solicit comments on the following topics:

- *Value.* Are there signs of change in a product's value? (See Principle 11 for forces to check.)
- *Competitors.* Any rumors about or value-changing actions by competitors?
- *Customer purchases.* Are customers changing their buying behaviors (swings in clients' interests, product demands, pricing needs, and so on)? What pricing initiatives have been successful in capitalizing on these changes?
- *What are the opportunities?* Is it possible to revise current pick-a-plan, versioning, and differential pricing tactics or implement new ones?

Periodic roundtable pricing events allow companies to benefit from some of the best available pricing insights—the experiences of and feedback from frontline employees. These meetings provide a forum for a team to exchange "company-centric" best-practice pricing tips with others. Teams leave a pricing roundtable feeling both relieved (it's cathartic to share challenges) and energized by the information, ideas, and support necessary to sharpen their pricing skills to generate a company's pricing windfall.

CREATE A WORKING ENVIRONMENT
THAT IS CONDUCIVE TO PROFITS AND GROWTH

For most companies, focusing on better pricing is a new strategy. This chapter provides a checklist of basics for companies to foster the business environment necessary to succeed in pricing for profits and growth. And while some of these principles seem obvious (similar to the hospital guideline "Ask the patient's name to make sure you have the right patient"), I do not know of a company that has incorporated all of these principles into its culture. If a company doesn't have a culture of profit in place, it is missing significant opportunities. After all, consider the downside of operating on the wrong patient because his or her name wasn't confirmed at the outset.

These culture-of-profit principles are easy to implement, are based on common sense, and have the potential to increase profits. However, the biggest benefit of implementing these principles is the sustainable pricing ecosystem that is created in a company. These principles promote synergy by feeding into and reinforcing each other. As a result, pricing becomes a proactive strategy, not a reactive one. The innate culture of a company continually motivates and focuses everyone on the goal of earning a pricing windfall.

KEY TAKEAWAYS

CREATE A CULTURE OF PROFIT

- A culture of profit is a business environment that supports and encourages everyone in a company to price for profits and growth.
- Creating a culture of profit involves implementing thirteen principles that are categorized in three groups: philosophies, foundations, and ongoing initiatives.
- Philosophies—break the myths. The following principles ensure that everyone is correctly thinking about price:

  - Principle 1: Set prices to capture the value customers place on a product.
  - Principle 2: It is possible to achieve both the largest market share *and* highest profits.
  - Principle 3: High-volume customers don't have to receive the lowest prices.
  - Principle 4: A discount today doesn't guarantee a premium tomorrow.
  - Principle 5: Higher operating margins are not a sign of better pricing.
  - Principle 6: An across-the-board discount is not the best response to the problem of reduced sales volume.

- Foundations—create confidence in the product. Two initiatives that encourage employees to highlight and capture the value of a product:

  - Principle 7: Create a value statement.
  - Principle 8: Reinforce that it is okay to earn profits.

- Ongoing initiatives—best practices for profit. Five actions that provide information, incentives, and support to help employees price for profits and growth:

  - Principle 9: Speak and sell in terms of net prices.
  - Principle 10: Organize and collect competitive information.
  - Principle 11: Monitor the value of products.
  - Principle 12: Incorporate profitability into compensation packages.
  - Principle 13: Host periodic pricing roundtables.

8

Make a Pricing Action Plan

START NOW

This book demonstrates that pricing has far more range than the conventional "raise it or lower it" usage. Chapters 1 to 7 presented four fundamental pricing strategies (value-based pricing, pick-a-plan, versioning, and differential pricing), fifty pricing tactics, two offensive pricing blossom strategies (B2C and B2B), six defensive pricing blossom strategy approaches (one for new entrants, two for recessions, and three for inflation), and thirteen culture-of-profit principles.

Figure 8-1 ■ Pricing Is a Multifaceted Strategy

Better pricing includes. . .

   Four fundamental pricing strategies

   Fifty pricing tactics

   Two offensive pricing blossom strategies

   Six defensive pricing blossom strategy approaches

   Thirteen culture-of-profit principles

Many of these concepts and tactics are used together in the pricing blossom strategy frameworks presented in Chapters 5 and 6. These frameworks provide guidance to create comprehensive offensive and defensive pricing strategies for every product. However, with so many concepts, strategies, tactics, and principles, it is fair to ask, "What can I do *right now* to start pricing for profits and growth?"

Better pricing is not an all-or-nothing strategy. Improvement initiatives can begin with implementing the basics and progress over time to develop a full-blown pricing strategy. It is often best to phase these in, as it takes time for employees to understand and master key concepts and strategies. Many multifunctional products (televisions and advanced computer-driven treadmills, for instance) have a Start Now button that allows users to immediately use and benefit from a product's basic capabilities. This chapter is the equivalent of a Start Now button for better pricing. It provides a manageable pathway to create a pricing blossom strategy and a culture of profit.

To create a comprehensive pricing strategy, I suggest assembling a team of senior executives and staff members involved with pricing in a company. This pricing team should include the chief financial officer (or representative), marketing managers, product managers, and frontline employees. Team members will provide insights on the pricing needs and behaviors of customers, devise and implement new strategies, and evangelize better pricing practices within an organization.

A pricing for profits and growth strategy can be designed and implemented in six sequential phases. Each phase has premeeting assignments, discusses fundamental pricing-blossom and culture-of-profit concepts, and results in tangible pricing actions. These phases can be gradually implemented over time, as well as used as an outline for a company off-site meeting to develop a comprehensive pricing strategy.

PHASE 1: DEVELOP A MIND-SET THAT
ENCOURAGES PRICING FOR PROFITS AND GROWTH

Pre-meeting reading: Introduction and culture-of-profit principles 1 and 9 (in Chapter 7).

The best way to evoke change is to emphasize the benefits that it will bring. Staff members have to understand and desire these benefits before they will make the efforts necessary to carry through a change. Pricing is a key variable in determining profits, as well as an important attribute in consumer purchase decisions. Just as important, small changes in price can lead to big profits. Highlighting the power of a 1% price increase (a company's 1% windfall) succinctly demonstrates the benefits of better pricing to staff members. It is important to explain to the team how to calculate a company's 1% windfall. This analysis employs straightforward arithmetic and real data. Assuming that demand remains constant, revenue from a 1% price increase is entirely additional profit. Thus, the percentage increase in operating profit from a 1% price increase is equal to:

$$\frac{1\% \text{ of revenue}}{\text{Current operating profits}} = 1\% \text{ windfall}$$

The benefits of a 1% price increase can also be expressed in terms of effects on market capitalization and additional profits (in dollars). There will generally be surprise about the big financial impact better pricing can have for their company.

What makes the 1% windfall credible is that this upside is calculated using data from a company's financial statement. In contrast, the projected benefits of most other business initiatives are based on many assumptions and cash flow projections. These less-than-transparent calculations are usually dismissed by staff members and Wall Street analysts, who feel they've heard it all before. Just as important, the changes necessary to reap a pricing windfall are achievable. After all, 1% is an attainable goal.

Once the power of better pricing is understood, some employees will proclaim, "We can easily raise our prices by 1%." At this point, it is important to note that in addition to a draconian across-the-board price increase, there are other, more customer-friendly strategies that can garner a pricing windfall. Make sure everyone understands that pricing tactics such as lowering overall prices, selective discounting, offering a variety of pricing plans, and providing customers with choices are win-win for both companies (who gain new profit) and customers (who benefit from lower prices and more options).

With the pricing team now engaged by the benefit of a 1% windfall, the next step is to ensure that members hold the same pricing assumptions and have the same goals. This involves gaining agreement on the following two culture-of-profit principles:

Set prices to capture the value that customers place on a product. Capturing value is usually the biggest mind-set change that needs to occur within a company. Since employees often hold divergent views on setting prices, this is a critical conversation to have with the pricing team. Once the intuition of value-based pricing is conveyed (using the umbrella, personal purchases, and success stories approach described in Chapter 7), team members typically understand and embrace this concept.

Speak in terms of net prices. From this point on, all selling prices listed on internal documents and discussed within a company should be framed in terms of net price. This helps frontline personnel understand and remain focused on the actual prices that buyers pay for their products.

Highlighting the amount of a company's 1% windfall (and the direct financial connection between price and profit), as well as reaching agreement on implementing value-based pricing and using net prices, creates the shared mind-set necessary to implement better pricing at a company.

Assignment to complete before the next meeting: Read Chapter 1 and culture-of-profit principles 7 and 8. Each participant should also construct a list of value-based attributes that make their products unique.

PHASE 2: SET A VALUE-BASED PRICE

This phase articulates a product's value and sets a value-based price. The first step of this process is to create a value statement for each product sold by a company. This involves soliciting input from employees across the company (or at least the pricing team) on attributes that make their product unique relative to the competition. These different attributes make up a company's value statement. A value statement is the basis for a product's sales pitch and the first step to determining a value-based price.

Once the attributes that differentiate a product are espoused in a value statement, the next step is to determine how much consumers are willing to pay for a product relative to its next-best alternative. Given the next-best alternative's price, how much more (or less) can be charged for the attributes that differentiate a product? Many shoppers will pay more for the brand name and quality of Birds Eye frozen corn relative to its next-best private-label alternative. But how much more: 10%, 25%, 50%? Estimates for this differential can be derived from market research, experienced judgment, and past price data. Chapter 1 describes the two approaches to calculate a value-based price for a product: one-on-one and multicustomer.

Once a value-based price has been determined, it is important to reinforce to the team that it is okay to earn profits. Frontline employees are often hesitant to implement value-based prices because they can't justify the price to themselves and have personal concerns about aggressively charging customers. Emphasizing a product's relative value and the idea that buyers find the product to be the best deal in the market builds the confidence and resolve to set prices that capture a product's value.

With the concept and implementation of value-based pricing set, this phase concludes by previewing the strategy of pricing discussed in the introduction to Part II. It is commonly recognized in many areas of business (product design, marketing, distribution, and so on) that the needs of potential customers differ. This is also true in pricing. To profit and grow from these differences, pricing strategies have to be implemented to serve customers' unique pricing needs. These differences include:

1. *Valuation.* Some customers are willing to pay more than others for a product.
2. *Product needs.* Customers have different product needs and desire different (place a greater value on certain) attributes.
3. *Pricing plans.* Customers may be interested in a product but refrain from buying because the selling strategy doesn't work for them.

It's these three fundamental differences that make pricing a strategy (with the goal of implementing a variety of tactics to serve as many customers as possible) instead of a search for a product's one "perfect" price. Companies have to understand the pricing needs of their potential customer base and implement a *series* of pricing tactics designed to attract (and profit from) as many of these different customers as possible.

Figure 8-2 ▪ Pricing Strategy Capitalizes on Customer Differences

Customer Difference	Pricing Tactics
Some customers willing to pay more than others	Differential pricing and versioning
Have unique product needs	Versioning
Desire different pricing plan	Pick-a-plan

Companies should think of their potential customer base as a giant jigsaw puzzle. Each new pricing tactic adds another customer segment piece to the puzzle. Normal Normans buy at full price (value-based price), Discount Davids are added by offering 10% off on Tuesday promotions (valuation), Noncommittal Nancys come for leases (pricing plans), and High-end Harrys buy premium versions (product needs). Employing differential pricing, versioning, and pick-a-plan pricing tactics adds the pricing-related segments necessary to complete a company's potential customer puzzle.

The next three phases create a series of pricing tactics to use for a product. Just to be clear, it is not always the case that all three strategies (pick-a-plan, versioning, and differential pricing) can be implemented for a product.

Assignment to complete before the next meeting: Read the introduction to Part II, Chapter 4, the differential pricing section of Chapter 5, and culture-of-profit principle 3. Participants should also list differential pricing tactics that are applicable to their products.

PHASE 3: IMPLEMENT DIFFERENTIAL PRICING BY OFFERING A RANGE OF PRICES

The primary goal of this session is for participants to devise a set of differential pricing tactics for each product. Understanding that customers have different valuations for a product, tactics should be implemented that segment and charge customers the price that they are willing to pay. Once a set of differential pricing tactics is identified, the next steps are to set a value-based price for each new tactic and conduct cannibalization checks. Consider the scenario of identifying senior citizens as a segment with lower valuations. A value-based analysis should be conducted to determine the discounted price to charge seniors. To prevent customers from other segments from using this discount (cannibalization), sellers can require proof-of-age identification to receive the discount. There are *always* two or three differential pricing tactics that can be implemented for a product.

This session should also discuss the often controversial third culture-of-profit principle, which holds that large-volume customers don't always have to receive the lowest prices. Strong demand from a customer reveals the high value that they place on a product, not necessarily a demand for the lowest price.

Assignment to complete before the next meeting: Read Chapter 3, the versioning section of Chapter 5, and culture-of-profit principles 4 and 5. Participants should list "good, better, and best" tactics, as well as unique needs versioning tactics that are applicable to their products.

PHASE 4: CREATE PRODUCT VERSIONS

Variations in a product's attributes can be used to capture different customer valuations, as well as generate growth through meeting unique needs. Higher margins are reaped from customers who purchase "better" and "best" products. Growth occurs from new customers attracted to good (price-sensitive) and best ("I only buy premium") versions, as well as those buying products that serve unique needs (Timex produces a variety of watches—its Ironman versions are targeted toward athletes). The team should create a versioning strategy for its products, as well as set value-based prices and conduct a cannibalization check for each new tactic. There's a *very good* chance of being able to offer two or three "good, better, and best" tactics and a *good* chance of offering one to three versions that meet unique customer needs.

This session concludes by breaking two common pricing myths. First, a discount today doesn't guarantee a premium tomorrow. While discounts induce trials, lower prices can also permanently devalue a product. As a result, it is often a challenge to persuade customers to pay full price for future purchases. The final myth to break is the often-held belief that higher operating margins are a sign of better pricing. A higher operating margin usually indicates that the average customer is paying a higher price. This means that there are opportunities to sell to price-sensitive customers. The best metric of better pricing initiatives is simply measuring if total profits are increasing.

Assignment to complete before the next meeting: Read Chapter 2, the pick-a-plan section of Chapter 5, and culture-of-profit principles 2 and 6. Participants should also list pick-a-plan tactics that are applicable to their products.

PHASE 5: PROVIDE PICK-A-PLAN SELLING OPTIONS

This pricing strategy session involves creating and implementing pick-a-plan tactics. Offering new pricing plans generates growth by meeting the pricing plan needs of segments. The team should brainstorm about new pricing plans that can activate dormant customers then set value-based prices for each new pricing plan and conduct cannibalization checks. Given that it is difficult to find appropriate new pricing plans, there is only a *fair* chance of being able to implement one or two pick-a-plan tactics.

After reviewing the comprehensive set of pricing tactics derived in Phases 1 through 5, two culture-of-profit principles should now be addressed. First, when facing lower demand, resist the temptation to implement an across-the-board discount. While it is understandable to focus on the weakened sales, don't forget that many customers continue to pay full price for the product. Instead of offering lower prices to all customers (including those who are currently paying full price), targeted discount tactics can be used to attract price-sensitive shoppers. Finally, it should be noted that it is possible to achieve both the highest market share and highest profits. The old-school thinking of a trade-off between price and market share is based on the notion that only one price can be set. In contrast, a pricing blossom strategy offers many prices, products, and plans that serve the most customers and earn the highest profits.

PHASE 6: CONTINUE BETTER
PRICING WITH ONGOING INITIATIVES

After Phases 1 through 5 have been undertaken, there are four on-going initiatives that should be implemented for a company to continue pricing for profits and growth.

Sales force compensation should be, in part, based on sales profit-ability. Volume-based commissions offer little incentive for salespeople to fight for what matters most to their companies: earning profits. Paying a sales force based on the profitability of sales transactions aligns their interests with those of the company.

Monitor the value of a product. Due to marketplace changes, the value of a product fluctuates over time. Monitoring these changes is critical to keep a product's price in line with its value over time.

Organize and collect information on the competition. Since a product's price is based on what the next-best alternative product charges, it is crucial to understand the pricing initiatives of competitors.

Speak in terms of net prices. A waterfall analysis should be under-taken to strip discounts from invoice prices. By focusing on the net prices that companies receive, this analysis reveals the true profitability of accounts. As a result, some accounts will be targeted for higher prices, while others will be better appreciated for the profits that they con-tribute to a company.

THE RESULTS OF PHASES 1 TO 6:
PRICING BLOSSOM STRATEGY AND A CULTURE OF PROFIT

By using this phased-in implementation process, a pricing blossom strategy will take form. While progressing through stages, a compa-ny's pricing team identifies unique customer segments with differing pricing needs and then offers tactics targeted to each of these segments. Pricing team insights (based on past experiences) on tactics, pricing, and cannibalization can be augmented by conducting additional market research.

In addition, by breaking myths, creating confidence in products, and implementing ongoing efforts, these six phases create a culture of profit. This culture supports staff members with the implementation of a pricing blossom strategy and keeps a company ahead of its rivals.

NOW IS THE TIME TO REAP A PRICING WINDFALL

At most companies today, pricing is a low-priority strategy. Prices are set for every product, of course, but generally by using methods that have been handed down from previous years and annual memos announcing cost-of-living increases that have nothing to do with capturing value. Since the upside of better pricing has not been clearly articulated, nor has a process to set prices been offered, it is understandable that pricing has been relegated to the status quo. Every day companies are missing profit opportunities because of their arcane pricing practices.

However, after reading this book, the situation is different. After a few calculations on data from their financial statements, managers know the 1% windfall benefits that better pricing can produce for their company. Instead of using the disparate pricing methods currently in place, companies now have a pricing blossom strategy framework that provides guidance on how to set prices that maximize profits, as well as the customer base of a company. In addition, this pricing blossom strategy framework provides defensive pricing responses to recession, inflation, and new competitors. Just as important, companies can foster a culture that creates a better pricing ecosystem that supports and encourages employees to price for profits and growth. As a result, companies can now convene an all-employee meeting and announce with credibility: "This is what better pricing will do for our bottom line, and this is how we can achieve our goals."

Figure 8-3
PRICING OPPORTUNITY CHECKLIST

How Well Does Your Company:	Well	Room for Improvement
1. Set prices that capture value?	❏	❏
2. Provide pick-a-plan options?	❏	❏
3. Sell versions?	❏	❏
4. Offer a series of prices to different customers?	❏	❏
5. Educate employees on the value of the products that they sell?	❏	❏
6. Encourage capturing the highest profits from every customer?	❏	❏
7. Break "within-company" pricing myths and behaviors which lower profits?	❏	❏
8. Reinforce the importance of pricing with continuing pricing discussions?	❏	❏
9. Keep a bottom-line focus by speaking in terms of net prices?	❏	❏
10. Promote better pricing with a supportive culture?	❏	❏

Company senior managers regularly exhort the value that they provide for consumers. Now it is time to focus on capturing the value of their products to benefit employees, shareholders, and, yes, customers. Virtually all of the fifty pricing tactics discussed in Chapters 2, 3, and 4 were framed in terms of satisfying a customer need. For these reasons, pricing should be a high-level strategy for every company.

Better pricing generates short-term and long-term profits. Since historically companies haven't focused on pricing, there are usually significant opportunities. Figure 8-3 provides a summary checklist to help managers identify areas of improvement at their companies. These opportunities generally don't require large investments and can start generating new profits almost immediately. Better pricing also creates a foundation that will produce future profits and growth. A strong pricing foundation will continue to generate profits as market conditions change and new products are developed. And best of all, the majority of the pricing concepts and tactics in a pricing blossom strategy are win-win for companies and their customers. Instead of one "take it or leave it" price, customers are offered choices of prices, versions, and pricing plans.

I have highlighted the pricing challenges and victories of managers in a wide variety of industries. Their dedication to capturing value and better serving their customers demonstrates the applicability of this book's concepts and strategies to every product and industry. These same techniques can reap a pricing windfall for your business too.

While reading this book, you've probably concluded that a 1% windfall is a conservative estimate of the amount that your company can achieve from better pricing. The benefits alone from employing value-based pricing *or* creating a culture of profit can surpass the 1% bar. I've found that implementing a comprehensive pricing blossom strategy usually generates additional profits (through growth and better margins) that are equivalent to a 3–5% pricing windfall.

With the frameworks, concepts, strategies, and tactics presented in this book, you are now equipped to price for profits and growth. As you are about to experience, small changes in price can lead to a financial windfall.

Acknowledgments

As I read the final draft of this manuscript, I can clearly see the influences of many people who went out of their way to help me with this endeavor. I listened, took notes, and the book is much stronger because of their assistance.

Betsy Whittemore is a great friend and tireless supporter. Always one step ahead of me ("where's the chapter?"), she provided superb advice. Thank you, Betsy.

Ben Loehnen offered excellent editorial guidance and I learned much from him. Echoing what others have said, Ben is very thorough and always right.

Rafe Sagalyn helped to develop the 1% concept and has generously guided this book to fruition.

George Eliades called me virtually every weekday to brainstorm on pricing ideas. His insights helped to sharpen this book. I appreciate our long-standing friendship.

Jan Eglen has been a first-class friend, supporter, and purveyor of wise comments. Our daily jousting provided much-needed humor to break the intensity of writing.

My longtime friend Patrick DeGraba retained his title of an "economist's economist." Patrick always cheerfully answered my questions.

Thanks to Matt Inman for his help and his all-encompassing abilities to make things happen.

I am very appreciative to Tom Neilssen for his great advice and always witty humor.

Steve Szaraz continued his role of close friend and advising editor. Steve is always able to improve my "best efforts."

Kirsten Sandberg always made time to provide top-notch strategic advice. I am glad that we have become good friends.

Bernie Jaworski has been a great friend and generous with his advice. The genesis of key framework concepts came from our brainstorming sessions in the "good old days."

I appreciate that fifteen years after my Ph.D. graduation, Rob Masson and Bob Frank continue to help and advise me.

Mark Kopelman was always available to provide generous assistance and engage in spirited discussions about new pricing ideas.

Ross McDonald continues to be an excellent Web developer and can be counted on to provide astute advice.

As with all research projects, I find it amazing how many people reached out to help with this book. Thanks to Jeff Eglen, Clint Briscoe, Wendy Knight, Jonathan Walker, Doc Kane, Andy Parece, Tom Copeland, Ken Li, and Steve Smith. Rosalie Lober provided valuable insights from the beginning. I am especially grateful to Katherine Myers for her friendship and for opening up big doors to the museum world.

Thank you to the following people for sharing their pricing stories, challenges, and victories with me: Olivier Biebuyck, Terrance Brennan, Peter Fuchs, Marc Geiger, Steve Good, Bjorn Hanson, Harold Holzer, Bruce Levinson, Chris MacAskill, Vince Rhoton, Fred Straus, Mike Straus, Paul Touw, David Tuckerman, and Larry Waxman.

My sincere thanks to my council of criticizers who pushed back on me and provided comments that improved the manuscript: Carol Miu, Scott Wallsten, Chris Maxwell, Craig Thompson, and Bob Cross.

Thanks to my longtime friends Gordon and Atusko Paddison, who are always available to talk, strategize, and offer wonderful hospitality.

Omar Saddick has been a bedrock friend for many years; he is a master problem solver.

Finally, I want to offer heartfelt thanks to the following long-standing friends for their support: Deborah Dupont, Kathy Ivanciw, Kathy Jocz, Gary Seigel, Linda Van Gelder, and Mike Yip.

Endnotes

Chapter : Introduction: The 1% Windfall

1. *2008 Annual Report for the Year Ending August 31, 2008, Costco Wholesale.* This calculation assumes that demand remains constant.

2. Michael Marn, Eric V. Roegner, and Craig C. Zwanda, *The Price Advantage* (New York: John Wiley & Sons, 2004), 5.

3. P/E ratio taken from Google Finance on July 24, 2009. The effects of a 1% increase in price on market capitalization assumes that a small change in price does not change quantity sold, the market did not anticipate this additional increase in profits, and that the 1% windfall gains are sustainable (not a one-time event).

4. According to Wal-Mart's 2008 10K Report, total revenues are $406 billion and its average tax rate is 34%. An extra 1% in revenue is $4 billion in extra profit; multiplied by the average tax rate (34%), that leads to an extra $2.6 billion in net profits. The approximate effect on Wal-Mart's market capitalization is $2.6 billion (additional net profit) multiplied by 14.56 (price-to-earnings ratio) = $37.9 billion.

5. Timothy Aeppel, "Seeking the Perfect Prices: CEO Tears Up the Rules," *Wall Street Journal*, March 27, 2007, 1.

6. Ibid.

7. "Set Us Free, Why Don't You," Pollstar.com, http://www.pollstar.com/news/viewnews.pl?NewsID=303; "Plug Pulled on Supremes Tour," *Oklahoma City Journal Record*, July 11, 2000.

8. Ibid.

9. Neil Strauss, "The Supremes May Be Ending the Tour," *New York Times*, July 11, 2000.

10. "Battered Carmakers Regain Shine in Summer of Record Sales," *Financial Times*, August 16, 2006, 36; Jennifer Saranow, "Employee Discounts Move Beyond Cars," *Wall Street Journal*, August 24, 2005, D1.

11. Chris Isidore, "Last Harry Potter Book Already No. 1," CNNMoney.com, February 2, 2007: http://money.cnn.com/2007/02/02/news/companies/harrypotter/index.htm.

12. Richard Gibson, "Franchisees Balk at Dollar Menu," *Wall Street Journal*, November 14, 2007.

13. Jeff Bailey, "Southwest Ends Open-Boarding Policy," *New York Times*, November 8, 2007.

14. Personal interview with Kevin Krone, June 27, 2008.

15. Susan Stellin, "Now Boarding Business Class," *New York Times*, February 26, 2008.

16. Postings from blogsouthwest.com.

Chapter 1: Capture Value by Thinking Like a Customer

1. Personal interview with Olivier Biebuyck, May 13, 2008.

2. Concrete is a mixture of cement and sand/gravel/crushed stone.

3. By "income effect," I mean that the consumer saved so much that they now have additional money (and desire) to purchase items that they otherwise might not purchase.

4. "Is There a Difference Between Tiffany, Costco Diamonds?" *Good Morning America*, October 9, 2005, http://abcnews.go.com/GMA/Moms/story?id=1197202.

5. Amy Culbertson, "Jamón Ibérico de Bellota Tastes Like Every Penny." *Star Telegram*, September 3, 2008.

6. This story was confirmed by Nordstrom on May 22, 2009.

7. Erik Holm, "Buffett Bidder Calls Lunch 'Investment in Our Future,'" *Bloomberg*, July 8, 2009.

8. Ibid.

9. A resource to learn more about conjoint analysis is *Getting Started with Conjoint Analysis* by Bryan K. Orme Madison, WI: (Research Publishers LLC, 2005).

10. Ann Zimmerman, "Wal-Mart Net Up 17% on Rebates, Bargain Hunters," *Wall Street Journal*, August 15, 2008, B1.

11. Chuck Martin, "Oprah Fans Scoop Up Graeters," *Cincinnati Enquirer*, June 4, 2002.

12. "ALG Repositions Vehicle Residual Values to Reflect High Fuel Costs," *Automotive Lease Guide*, July 28, 2008.

13. Personal interview with Chris MacAskill, August 13, 2008.

14. Jessica Guynn, "A Family Focused Business," *Los Angeles Times*, December 24, 2007.

Chapter 2: Pick-a-Plan

1. "Termites Likely to Flourish in Warm Spring Weather," National Pest Management Association, Inc., March 10, 2009.
2. Debbie Arrington, "Checklist: In the Garden, In the Home," *Sacramento Bee*, April 25, 2009.
3. Personal interview with Steve Good, September 17, 2008.
4. "Timeshare Industry Continues Strong Growth with 2005 Sales of 8.6 Billion," *Business Wire*, September 25, 2006.
5. Ibid.
6. Carol Sottili, "Timeshares Aren't What They Used to Be. Trust Us. We Sat Through Six Pitches in Two Days," *Washington Post*, December 17, 2006.
7. Jeffrey Selingo, "Hotels Shake Up Timeshare Act," *New York Times*, April 10, 2007.
8. "Consumer Reports 10 Best and Worst Cars for Depreciation," *Chatham Journal Weekly*, November 28, 2006.
9. Ibid.
10. John D. Stoll, Liz Rappaport, and Matthew Dolan, "GM, Ford Scale Back Leases as Era Ends," *Wall Street Journal*, July 30, 2008.
11. John D. Stoll and Sharon Terlep, "Lease Cutbacks Leave Cadillacs Idling," *Wall Street Journal*, September 22, 2009.
12. John D. Stoll and Matthew Dolan, "Ford's Finance Arm Tightens Lease Terms on Trucks, SUVs," *Wall Street Journal*, July 29, 2008.
13. Ibid.
14. Sarah Nassauer, "Enterprise Plans to Expand Car Sharing Business in U.S.," *Wall Street Journal*, October 1, 2008.
15. Miguel Helft, "We Rent Movies, So Why Not Textbooks?" *New York Times*, July 5, 2009.
16. David Koenig, "Blockbuster Finish for Movie-Rental Co," *USA Today*, March 7, 2008; Melissa Korn and Kathy Shwiff, "Netflix Adds Subscribers, Boosts Net," *Wall Street Journal*, July 24, 2009.
17. "Schilling's Deal with Red Sox Worth $8M Plus Incentives," ESPN.com News Services, November 7, 2007.
18. Steve Silva, "Done Deal," Boston.com, November 6, 2007. However, Schilling ended up injured and did not play in 2008. The Red Sox had not taken out an insurance policy and thus had to pay out $8 million. See Gordon Edes, "Schilling Pact Not Insured," *Boston Globe*, February 11, 2008.

19. Debra Cassens Weiss, "Holland & Knight Tries Success Fees, Considers Ousting Unproductive Partners," *ABA Journal*, July 16, 2008.

20. Jonathan Karp, "Condo-Minimum," *Wall Street Journal*, September 10, 2008.

21. Ibid.

22. Ibid.

23. Jill Lawless, "Hirst Auction Breaks Record at Sotheby's," Associated Press, September 16, 2007.

24. David Lowe, "I'm Proud Damien Can Sell My £90 Shark for Millions," *The Sun*, September 19, 2008.

25. Chad Terhune, "New Insurance Plan Has Novel Twist: Get Sick, Buy More," *Wall Street Journal*, September 14, 2007.

26. Sandhya Bathija, "Small Firms Turning to Flat Fees for Profits," *The National Law Journal*, March 29, 2007.

27. Tamara Loomis, "The Power of One," *Corporate Counsel*, September 1, 2008.

28. Robert Gavin, "Heating Oil Users Face Costly Winter," *Boston Globe*, November 1, 2007.

29. "Restaurants Spurn Food Contracts for Spot Market," *Cattlenetwork*, August 4, 2008.

30. Bruce Mohl, "Price-cap Plans for Oil Can Be Tough to Gauge." *Boston Globe*, October 2, 2005.

31. Brian Stelter, "To Curb Traffic on the Internet, Access Providers Consider Charging by the Gigabyte," *New York Times*, June 15, 2008.

32. Susan Spielberg, "Chains on Tightrope to Balance Inventories, Consumer Demand," *Nation's Restaurant News*, August 9, 2004.

33. John Donovan and Charles Herman, "Costco Cashes in on Bargain-Hungry Shoppers," ABC News, May 29, 2008.

34. Ashley Parker, "Tightening the Beltway, The Elite Shop Costco," *New York Times*, November 25, 2007.

35. Steven Greenhouse, "How Costco Became the Anti-Wal-Mart," *New York Times*, July 17, 2005.

36. 2008 *Annual Report for the Year Ending August 31, 2008, Costco Wholesale*. More precisely, its operating profits equal membership fees plus approximately 0.6% of percent of revenues.

37. 2008 *Annual Report for the Year Ending August 31, 2008, Costco Wholesale*.

38. William M. Bulkeley, "Kodak CEO Bets Big on Printers," *Wall Street Journal*, July 8, 2009.

39. Ibid.

40. Miguel Bustillo and Ann Zimmerman, "Retailers Brace for Lean Holidays," *Wall Street Journal*, October 9, 2008.

41. Best Buy F1Q08 Earnings Call Transcript, June 17, 2008: http://seeking alpha.com/article/81699-best-buy-f1q09-qtr-end–5–31–08-earnings-call-transcript?page=–1&find=%24999.

42. For more information, see http://www.williams-sonomainc.com/inv/fpr/index. cfm?listPressReleaseDetails=1&pressReleaseID=A21371DD-EA98–442A–890300CD65C977FA.

43. Gillian Livingston, "Beware the No-Pay Deal; Failure to Pay on Date Can Cost You Big Time," *The Hamilton Spectator*, January 10, 2003.

44. Kate Linebaugh, "AutoNation Layoff Guarantee," *Wall Street Journal*, March 19, 2009.

45. Miguel Bustillo, "Layaway Is Making a Comeback," *Wall Street Journal*, October 22, 2008.

46. "Kmart's Hot Xmas Idea: Layaway," *Brandweek*, November 20, 2008.

47. Susan Sachs, "Immigrants See Path to Riches in Phone Cards," *New York Times*, August 11, 2002.

48. Brian Grow, "Talk Isn't So Cheap on a Phone Card," *BusinessWeek*, July 23, 2007.

49. Personal interview with Paul Touw, September 9, 2008.

50. Personal interview with Peter Fuchs, August 8, 2008.

51. Jeff Burger, "XOJET's Paul Touw Touts Virtues of Two-Model Fleet," *Business Jet Traveler*, April 1, 2008.

Chapter 3: Versioning

1. Personal interview with Terrance Brennan, September 23, 2008.

2. Ruth Reichl, "Restaurants," *New York Times*, March 15, 1996.

3. Frank Bruni, "Birds Still Soar, and They're Not Alone," *New York Times*, November 8, 2006; Steve Cuozzo, "Mr. Met: Picholine Revamps for Opera Crowd," *New York Post*, September 27, 2006; Gael Greene, "Picholine," *New York Magazine*, September 24, 2006.

4. Elizabeth Campbell, "Starbucks Tries Brew with a More Premium Price," *Boston Globe*, August 26, 2008.

5. For more information, see http://www.toro.com/home/mowers/index.html

6. Della de Lafuente, "Premium M&M's Make Fashionable Debut," *Adweek*, September 8, 2008.

7. For more information, see http://www.massport.com/logan/parki_passgold. html

8. Randy Diamond, "For a Price, It's Fine to Cut in Line," *Tampa Tribune*, October 15, 2005.

9. "Skip to the Head of the Line, for a Price," *Washington Post*, March 19, 2007.

10. Randy Diamond, "For a Price, It's Fine; To Cut in Line."

11. Matt Ritchell and Ashlee Vance, "In the Age of Impatience, Cutting PC Start Time," *New York Times*, October 25, 2008.

12. *Amtrak Annual Report 2008*, page 7.

13. Lavonne Kukendall, "Tale of the Tape: Allstate Sees Hard '08 But a Price-War End," *Dow Jones News Service*, April 4, 2008.

14. Personal interview with Ray Magliozzi, November 5, 2008.

15. For more information, see http://www.bls.gov/cpi/cpifacaf.htm

16. Ken Barnes, "Digital Single Tracks Soar in Sales as Albums Drop," *USA Today*, January 3, 2008.

17. "Sonic Reports Record Second Quarter 2008 Earnings," Sonic Press Release, March 24, 2008.

18. Lisa Rein, "Off-Peak Laundry? Pricing Power by the Hour," *Washington Post*, December 12, 2007.

19. Jeremiah McWilliams, "Private-label Makers Strive to Brand Their Bigger Rivals," *St. Louis Dispatch*, August 8, 2008.

20. Sonia Reyes, "Saving Private Labels," *Brandweek*, May 8, 2006.

21. Ibid.

22. Eric Felten, "The Single-Malt Independents," *Wall Street Journal*, July 12, 2008.

23. "Report: Health Costs Rise, Coverage Wanes," CBS News, September 24, 2008.

24. Prices at Morrell & Company checked on June 2, 2009.

25. Jeremy M. Peters, "Fewer Bites, Fewer Calories, Lot More Profit," *New York Times*, July 7, 2007.

26. Ibid.

27. "Why You Don't Need an Extended Warranty," *Consumer Reports*, November 2007.

28. Terrence O'Hara, "Unwarranted: In Most Cases, Extended Product Service Plans Don't Benefit Customers," *Washington Post*, October 1, 2006.

29. Matthew Karnitschnig, "Book-of-the-Month to Turn a New Page," *Wall Street Journal*, April 10, 2007.

30. Ibid.

31. Martin Moyland, "Time to Bundle Up Your Telecom Bills," Minnesota Public Radio, April 20, 2007.

32. Ibid.

33. This pricing data is for 2008 models.

34. Thomas Jaffe, "In a Pickle," Forbes.com, March 8, 1999.

35. Katharine Q. Seelye, "The 2000 Campaign: The Vice President; Under Attack, Gore Reshapes Censure of Drug Industry," *New York Times*, September 21, 2000.

36. For more information, see http://www.wma.com/bb_king/summary
37. 2007 Pollstar Tour Report for B.B. King.
38. Personal interview with Marc Geiger, October 27, 2008.

Chapter 4: Differential Pricing

1. Research was conducted on June 5, 2009, for the Omni Berkshire Hotel in New York City for a June 27 to July 2, 2009, visit.
2. This rate was claimed on the hotel price resource website biddingfortravel. com: http://biddingfortravel.yuku.com/topic/89226/t/4-MTE-Omni-Berkshire-Place-136-6-27-7-2.html
3. Personal interview with Bjorn Hanson, November 5, 2009.
4. Brian Grow and Rishi Chhatwal, "The Great Rebate Runaround," *Business-Week*, December 5, 2005.
5. Ibid.
6. Teresa F. Lindeman, "Shoppers Come Out in Full Force," *Pittsburgh Post Gazette*, November 25, 2006.
7. Cheryl Lu-Lien Tan, Gary McWilliams, and Amy Merrick, "After Rush, Retailers Try New Shopping Lures," *Wall Street Journal*, November 26, 2007.
8. Anjali Cordeiro, "Consumers Pick Up Clip of Coupons," *Wall Street Journal*, September 25, 2008.
9. Since stores in other geographic areas or Internet retailers do not offer the same value, most price-match guarantees will not honor those prices.
10. Anne T. Coughlan and David A. Soberman, "Strategic Segmentation Using Outlet Malls," *International Journal of Research in Marketing* 22, 1 (2005): 61–86.
11. Lauren Foster, "Coach Sales Strategy Is in the Bag," *Financial Times*, April 18, 2006.
12. Stephanie Saul, "More Generics Slow the Surge in Drug Prices," *New York Times*, August 8, 2007.
13. Ibid.
14. For more information, see http://www.intel.com/technology/mooreslaw
15. Damon Darlin, "Why Appliances Buck the Trend and Cost More," *New York Times*, March 11, 2006.
16. Andrew Pollack, "U.S. Approves Type of Corn That May Cut Pesticide Use," *New York Times*, February 26, 2003.
17. Crop Production: *Fiscal Year 2002 National Program Annual Report, United States Department of Agriculture.*
18. Event Brief of Q3 2008 Monsanto Company Earnings Conference Call, Voxant Fair Disclosure Wire, June 25, 2008.

19. Fran Hawthorne, "AARP's Invite Presents a Wrinkle for Some," *New York Times*, April 11, 2006.

20. Richard B. Schmitt, "Latest Discount From AARP is on Lawyers," *Wall Street Journal*, November 7, 1996.

21. "Burger King Introduces Value Meals," *QSR Magazine*, April 23, 2001.

22. Ibid.

23. Portia Smith, "Competition Drives Prices in Local Area Stores," Knight Ridder/Tribune Business News, March 10, 2005.

24. Ibid.

25. "Gasoline Pricing Questions and Answers from Chevron," PR Newswire, May 4, 1998.

26. James Niccolai, "Sony Losing Big Money on PS 3 Hardware," *PC World*, November 16, 2006.

27. Carolyn Said, "Ink. Inc.," *San Francisco Chronicle*, July 26, 2004.

28. Dean Takahashi, "California Father-Son Cartridge Franchise Takes on Hewlett-Packard," Forbes.com, July 13, 2004.

29. Thanks to Lyra Research (www.lyra.com) for sharing this information with me.

30. Chris Anderson, *The Long Tail: Why the Future of Business Is Selling Less of More* (New York: Hyperion, 2006), 23.

31. Each of these films ranks in the top twenty of all-time box office receipts and in total they have earned close to $3 billion worldwide. Personal interview with David Tuckerman, June 17, 2008.

32. Bruce Mohl, "Now Showing: Epic Cost of Cinema Snacks," *Boston Globe*, March 2, 2007.

33. Richard Thaler, "Mental Accounting and Consumer Choice," *Marketing Science* 4 (1985): 199–214.

Chapter 5: Create a Pricing Blossom Strategy

1. Bruce Horovitz, "Six Strategies Marketers Use to Get Kids to Want Stuff Bad," *USA Today*, November 22, 2006.

2. Motoko Rich and Brad Stone, "A New World: Scheduling E-Books," *New York Times*, July 14, 2009.

3. The Metropolitan Museum of Art, *One Hundred Thirty-Eighth Annual Report of the Trustees for the Fiscal Year July 1, 2007 through June 30, 2008*, November 12, 2008.

4. Ibid.

5. Personal interview with Harold Holzer, August 13, 2008.

6. The Metropolitan Museum of Art.

7. "Landmark *Age of Rembrandt* Exhibition Puts Met's Entire Dutch Paintings

Collection of 228 Works on View in September," press release from the Metropolitan Museum of Art, September 7, 2007.

8. Holland Cotter, "A Golden Age Gobbled Up by the Gilded Age," *New York Times*, September 18, 2007.

Chapter 6: Defensive Pricing: Recession, Inflation, and New Competitors

1. Personal interview with Bruce Levinson, December 22, 2008.

2. Ibid.

3. Matt Krantz, "Markets Fall in 2008 Was Worst in Seven Decades," *USA Today*, January 2, 2009.

4. Ray A. Smith, "Discounts Fail to Save Retailers' Holiday," *Wall Street Journal*, December 31, 2008.

5. Ellen Simon, "Retailers' Holiday Sales Drop by at Least 5.5%," *International Business Times*, December 25, 2008.

6. "Campbell's Soup Reports Jump in Sales and Profits," Associated Press, September 11, 2008 and "McDonald's Same Store Sales Jump in November," *Chicago Sun Times*, December 8, 2008.

7. Ibid.

8. Reuters, "Factbox—Top 10 Best and Worst Performers," December 31, 2008.

9. "Supermarkets News . . . Supermarkets Bloom," *FMCG & Retail News*, January 2, 2009.

10. Jonathan Birchall and Elizabeth Rigby, "P&G Chief Relaxed About Meeting Goals," *Financial Times*, June 26, 2008.

11. Timothy Aeppel, "Guitar Maker Revives No-Frills Act from '30s," *Wall Street Journal*, July 6, 2009.

12. Ibid.

13. Becky Yerak, "Allstate: Auto Insurance Policy Holders Reducing Coverage in Recession," *Chicago Tribune*, January 30, 2009.

14. Jane Black, "The Fixe Is In," *Washington Post*, December 31, 2008.

15. "McDonald's to Launch Bigger, $4 Angus Burgers," *USA Today*, July 2, 2009.

16. For more information, please see: http://www.airlines.org/economics/energy

17. Andrew Edwards and Kevin Kingsbury, "Prices for 3M Optical Films Will Fall for Some Customers," *Wall Street Journal*, October 20, 2007.

18. Ibid.

19. Glenn Collins, "As Business Gets Lean, A Big King Dares Big Mac," *New York Times*, August 28, 1997.

20. Ibid.

Chapter 7: Create a Culture of Profit

1. Alex B. Haynes, Thomas G. Weiser, William R. Berry, Stuart R. Lipsitz, Abdel-Hadi S. Breizat, E. Patchen Dellinger, Teodoro Herbosa, Sudhir Joseph, Pascience L. Kibatala, Marie Carmela M. Lapitan, Alan F. Merry, Krishna Moorthy, Richard K. Reznick, Bryce Taylor, and Atul A. Gawande, " A Surigical Safety Checklist to Reduce Morbidity and Mortality in a Global Population," *The New England Journal of Medicine* (January 29, 2009): 491–499.

2. Mike Stobbe, "Study: Basic Checklist Cuts Surgical Deaths in Half," Associated Press, January 14, 2009.

3. Matt Richtel, "Even at Megastores, Hagglers Find No Price is Set in Stone," *New York Times*, March 23, 2008.

4. Michael V. Marn, Eric V. Roegner, and Craig C. Zawada, *The Price Advantage* (New York: John Wiley & Sons, 2004), 5.

5. Ibid., 25.

Index

About the Author

RAFI MOHAMMED is the founder of Culture of Profit LLC, a business consulting company that works with companies on their pricing strategy. He has worked on pricing issues at the Federal Communications Commission during the deregulation of the telecommunications industry, testified as a pricing expert in front of public policy commissions, and was formerly a consultant at Monitor Group. Rafi also holds the title of Batten Fellow at the University of Virginia's Darden Graduate School of Business (in residence, Spring 2001).

He is the author of *The Art of Pricing* and coauthor of *Internet Marketing: Building Advantage in a Networked Economy.* Rafi's pricing articles have been published in leading journals, including the *Rand Journal of Economics,* and he is a frequent commentator on pricing issues to the media

Rafi was born in Milwaukee and raised in Cincinnati. He is an economics graduate of Boston University, the London School of Economics and Political Science, and Cornell University (Ph.D.).

His website is www.pricingforprofit.com.